The Atlas of ANCIENT EGYPT

Published in the United States in 2000
by PETER BEDRICK BOOKS
A division of NTC/Contemporary Publishing Group, Inc.
4255 West Touhy Avenue, Lincolnwood (Chicago), Illinois
60646-1975 U.S.A.

The Atlas of Ancient Egypt was created and produced by
McRae Books Srl, via de' Rustici, 5 – Florence (Italy)
e-mail: mcrae@tin.it

Text Neil Morris
Main Illustrations Paola Ravaglia, Studio Stalio (Alessandro Cantucci, Fabiano
Fabbrucci, Andrea Morandi, Ivan Stalio), Matteo Chesi and Lorenzo Cecchi

Picture research: Anne McRae
Graphic Design Marco Nardi
Editing Cath Senker
Layout and cutouts Adriano Nardi and Ornella Fassio

Color separations Litocolor, Florence

Printed in China
International Standard Book Number: 0-87226-610-9

00 01 02 03 15 14 13 12 11 10 9 8 7 6 5 4 3 2

THE ATLAS OF
ANCIENT
EGYPT

Neil Morris

Illustrations Paola Ravaglia, Matteo Chesi,
Studio Stalio (Fabiano Fabbrucci, Alessandro Cantucci,
Andrea Morandi, Ivan Stalio)

PETER BEDRICK BOOKS
NEW YORK

Contents

Osiris, the god of death and resurrection, as depicted in the tomb of Ramesses I in the Valley of the Kings. The god wears his distinctive tall white crown with two plumes and carries the royal crook and flail. The dead king was always associated with Osiris, whose green skin represents resurrection.

These limestone molds from the Coptic period were used to make small sacred images for figurines and amulets.

Wooden model of a man cooking beef. He is also using a fan to keep the fire going. Beef was the favorite meat among those Egyptians who could afford it.

Royal princesses – daughters of Amenhotep IV (ruled 1350–34 BC) and his wife Nefertiti – from a wall decoration at the royal palace at el-Amarna. In the fifth year of his reign the king changed his name from Amenhotep ("Amun is content") to Akhenaten ("one who is useful to Aten"), when he made the sun-god Aten the center of worship (see pages 31 and 33).

Chronology of Ancient Egypt

PREDYNASTIC ERA *up to 3150 BC*		
THE FIRST DYNASTIES *3150–2686 BC*		
THE OLD KINGDOM *2686–2181 BC*		
FIRST INTERMEDIATE PERIOD *2181–2040 BC*		
THE MIDDLE KINGDOM *2040–1782 BC*		
SECOND INTERMEDIATE PERIOD *1782–1570 BC*		
THE NEW KINGDOM *1570–1070 BC*		
THIRD INTERMEDIATE PERIOD *1070–525 BC*		
THE LATE PERIOD *525–332 BC*		
GREEK AND ROMAN PERIOD *332 BC – AD 641*		

Painted wooden head of the childlike sun-god emerging from a lotus flower, from the tomb of the boy-king Tutankhamun (ruled 1334–25 BC).

Wooden shabti of the "mistress of the house" Urni, dating from the New Kingdom period, with hieroglyphic inscriptions in black ink. Such funerary figurines were placed in tombs to attend to the deceased in the afterlife.

Introduction

This book traces the course of almost four thousand years of civilization in the valley of the Nile River. Ancient Egypt was one of the most long-lasting civilizations in the ancient world, and its people left behind many reminders of their amazing achievements. Some of their creations are among the most famous wonders of the ancient world: the Great Pyramid at Giza, with its secrets and mysteries; Tutankhamun's tomb in the Valley of the Kings; and the Rosetta stone, which modern archeologists used to decipher Egyptian hieroglyphs. Many more temples and tombs, along with their well-preserved coffins, mummies, wall paintings, and statues, have told us a great deal about the ways of the pharaohs and their royal families, as well as their important gods and goddesses. Yet the lives and beliefs of ordinary Egyptians are equally interesting, from the farmers along the Nile who used the annual flood to help feed and develop this great civilization, to the villagers who built and decorated the royal cemeteries. This book explores the complete history and geography of the great civilization of ancient Egypt.

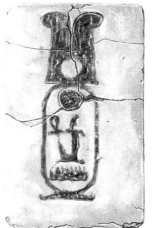

Two glazed faience tiles show the royal names of King Seti I (ruled 1291–78 BC), the second ruler of the 19th Dynasty, inside ovals called cartouches. The tiles were buried in the foundations of Seti's mortuary temple.

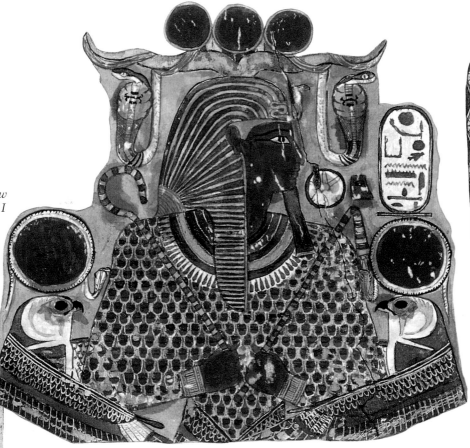

Wall painting of Amenhotep I (ruled 1551–24 BC) with all the symbols of Egyptian kingship. Amenhotep was the second king of the brilliant New Kingdom. He was the first pharaoh to build a mortuary temple some distance away from his burial place.

Soon after 2000 BC, during the Middle Kingdom period, coffins were made in this human shape rather than being simply rectangular. They were highly decorated on the inside, often showing images of gods and goddesses.

Predynastic Egypt

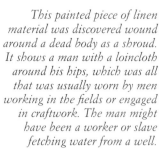

This painted piece of linen material was discovered wound around a dead body as a shroud. It shows a man with a loincloth around his hips, which was all that was usually worn by men working in the fields or engaged in craftwork. The man might have been a worker or slave fetching water from a well.

Our human ancestors have been living in the Nile valley since early prehistoric times. Archeologists have found hand axes at Abu Simbel, the site of later temples, that date back about 700,000 years.

Unfortunately for modern archeologists, however, the annual Nile floods washed away most traces of prehistoric human life. We know that by about 10,000 BC groups of people were wandering around the fertile region beside the Nile River, hunting, fishing and gathering roots, seeds, and berries. Around 5500 BC these people started to farm crops and, slightly later, to herd animals such as goats and sheep. Their settlements grew into small villages, which then made alliances, and during the fourth millennium BC formed two separate lands. We call the land around the lowlands of the Nile delta Lower Egypt, and the land farther up the narrow Nile valley Upper Egypt. Each land was a kingdom with its own capital. We know little about these people's kings, but they must have struggled for centuries to gain power over larger and larger groups of people. The time up until about 3100 BC is known as the predynastic period because it came before the recognized dynasties, or series of ruling families, who later reigned over a unified Egypt.

This statue of a woman dates from about 3500 BC. Made of unfired clay, it is one of many small female statues produced by prehistoric people in Egypt (and in many other places too). The body's female shape has been accentuated and historians think that these figures were used as idols to worship the female ability to give birth. They are also called "mother goddesses."

Hunters and gatherers

The earliest people to live in the Nile valley moved around the region, hunting animals and gathering plants. They also fished in the river. In prehistoric times the region changed with the climate; at one time there were swamps and grasslands where now there is the desert land of the Sahara. This environment would then have been able to support much more wildlife than in later times.

Sailing on the Nile

Wood is scarce in Egypt and the earliest boats were made of reeds tied together. The paddles were also made of reeds. In time the Egyptians learned to shape the local acacia trees into wooden boats. They were among the earliest people in the world to use a sail. At first they used a leafy frond set in the bows (see Naqada I vase, next page), then they learned to weave reeds or leaves together to make a real sail.

Black and red lands

The ancient Egyptians called the fertile region around the river valley of the Nile *kemet*, which means "the black land." This was because of the rich, dark silt that was spread across the land every year by the floodwaters of the Nile, which the Egyptians called simply "the river" (*iterw*). They called themselves *remetch en kemet*, "people of the black land," and it seems that they associated the color black with birth and life. The fertile landscape was surrounded by dry, barren desert, which was known to them as *deshret*, "the red land."

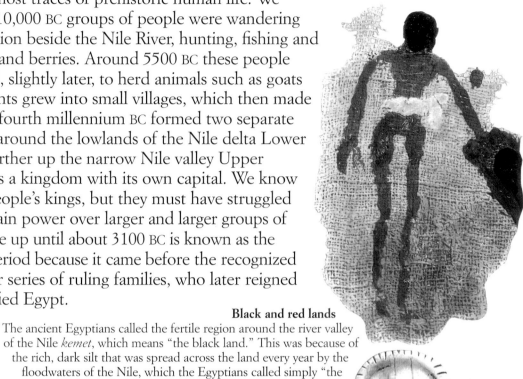

Early Egyptian hunters made stone-cutting tools like the ones shown here. Their sharpened edges were used to cut meat, skin animals, and to scrape the pelts.

This flint knife has a rippled blade and an elegantly carved ivory handle. It is typical of knives produced during the Naqada II period just prior to the unification of Egypt.

Tiny clay model of a boat carrying a passenger, from about 3000 BC.

Although this looks like a modern statue of a young woman at the beach in a bikini and wearing sunglasses, it was actually carved by the ancient Egyptians over 6,000 years ago. Like the other female statue (above), it was probably a cult figure or a mother goddess.

CLIMATE AND AGRICULTURE IN PREDYNASTIC EGYPT

ATLAS MOUNTAINS
MEDITERRANEAN SEA
Nile delta
RED SEA
S A H A R A
Nile River
S A H E L

Mediterranean
Desert
Sahel and steppe
Woodland savanna
Tropical rain forest
Upland and mountain
Sheep and goats
Cattle
Earliest cereal cultivation

Early agriculture

By about 5500 BC people in the village communities near the Nile were cultivating their own crops of wheat and barley, rather than simply gathering cereal grasses as they found them. At first, farmers probably grew enough just for themselves and their families, depending on how big the annual flood and resulting harvest were. The rich soil could usually support at least two crops a year. Villagers kept long-horned cattle for their meat and milk, and sheep and goats also provided wool and hide. The early farmers soon learned to dig canals, which were flooded by the Nile and then blocked off to store the river's water.

The new stone age (neolithic)

Egyptologists divide the neolithic in Egypt (about 5500 until 3100 BC), into three periods. The earliest is called Badarian, after a site in Upper Egypt where the people raised sheep, goats, and pigs, wore linen clothes (perhaps sewn by the men, since bone needles were only found in male graves) and jewelry, and produced female statues and black-topped vases. This was followed by the Naqada periods I and II. The Naqada I people had the same technology as the earlier Badarians but they also kept donkeys and cattle, and used bricks to build their houses. During Naqada II they developed even further and were influenced by neighboring peoples in Syria and Mesopotamia.

Above: wooden model boat and arrow from a predynastic burial.

This necklace is made of shells collected in the Nile River. The bracelet, part of a set with a necklace, is made from carved bone and blue-green faience beads.

Below: this man, known as "Ginger" for the color of his hair, was buried in predynastic times.

This large vase with dark figures is typical of the Naqada II period. It shows a boat with gazelles, a bird, and a woman with her arms raised. The double arrow symbol in the middle may represent a god.

Below: black-topped vase made in about 4500 BC during the Badarian period.

Predynastic burials

During this early period the Egyptians buried their dead directly in the desert sand, curled up on their left sides. The heat of the sand drew the body's moisture from it, so preventing decay. Grave goods, including pottery, palettes, jewelry, figurines, and personal possessions, were placed in the tomb around the body.

Hippopotamus horns, either hollowed out or flattened and carved, like the ones shown here, were frequently placed in tombs. The Egyptians probably thought they had magic powers to help the dead.

These baskets were found in predynastic graves. They may have contained food for the afterlife.

Below: red bowl with two white crocodiles, typical of the Naqada I style of pottery.

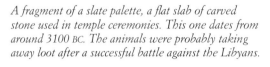

A fragment of a slate palette, a flat slab of carved stone used in temple ceremonies. This one dates from around 3100 BC. The animals were probably taking away loot after a successful battle against the Libyans.

The First Dynasties

The First Dynasty of kings began around 3150 BC with Narmer, who was associated with the legendary King Menes as well as the falcon-god Horus, the main god of kingship. The second king, whose name Aha means "the fighter," may have been Narmer's son. Over a period of about 200 years a series of probably eight kings ruled over the newly unified Egypt. About 2950 BC King Den's mother, Merneith, may also have ruled as a regent until he was old enough to take power. During the Second Dynasty (from about 2890–2686 BC) there were up to seven kings, ending with Khasekhemwy, who had an elaborate tomb nearly 115 feet long near a large mud-brick funeral enclosure. Most of the little we know about the lives of the early kings was gained from their tombs. Khasekhemwy's tomb, for example, was the earliest to include a statue of the king and to contain vessels made of bronze, which began to replace the earlier copper.

King Scorpion

One of the early rulers of Upper Egypt, before the two kingdoms were ruled as one, has been given the name King Scorpion. This is because he is shown with a scorpion on a limestone macehead (right) found in a tomb at Abydos. The pear-shaped piece of stone was attached to the end of a wooden rod to make a weapon called a mace. It dates from about 3150 BC, and it shows the early king wearing the white crown and apparently digging an irrigation canal with the help of attendants.

White, red, and double crown

The king of the two unified lands wore a double crown. This cleverly combined the cone-shaped white crown of Upper Egypt and the more open red crown of Lower Egypt.

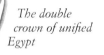

The double crown of unified Egypt

The red crown of Lower Egypt.

The white crown of Upper Egypt.

Ivory statuette of a First Dynasty king wearing the white crown of Upper Egypt and a decorated ceremonial robe.

First king of the First Dynasty

King Narmer was the first to rule both lands of Egypt, some time around 3150 BC. Many scholars believe that he was the same person as Menes, known in legend as the first human ruler, and that he unified Egypt and founded its capital, Memphis. On one side of a mudstone palette that was found intact (right), Narmer is shown wearing the crown of Upper Egypt. He is about to strike a foreigner. On the other side of the palette (below), he wears the crown of Lower Egypt and is shown marching with standard-bearers toward a group of beheaded prisoners. Historians list Narmer as the first king of the Egyptian First Dynasty.

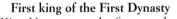

Above: Narmer Palette, side A.

Below: Narmer Palette, side B (detail).

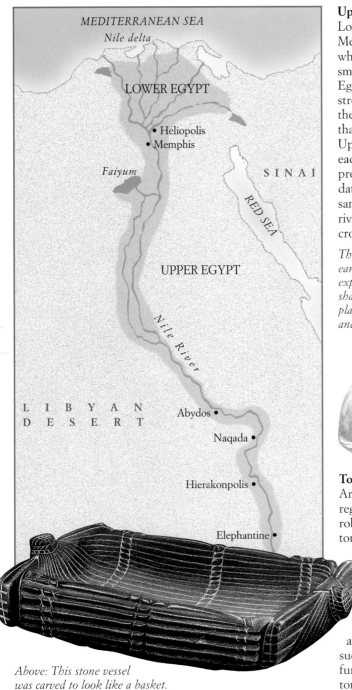

Upper and Lower Egypt

Lower Egypt covered the area from the Mediterranean Sea to just below Memphis, where the Nile River fans out into several smaller channels that make up its delta. Upper Egypt covered the area south of Memphis, stretching along the Nile valley to Aswan and the island of Elephantine, a distance of more than 435 miles. From early dynastic times, Upper Egypt was divided into 22 provinces, each with its own capital. Lower Egypt had 20 provinces, which may have originated at a later date. In this delta region, villages were built on sandy ridges between the small branches of the river. The villagers reclaimed more land for crops as time passed.

This First Dynasty stone vase (right) has a gilded rim. The early Egyptians quarried stone in the desert and became expert at working with hard materials. They also carved and shaped more delicate items, such as these lion-shaped ivory playing pieces, as well as necklaces and other jewelry from shells and precious stones.

Tombs

Archeologists have excavated many tombs throughout the whole region of ancient Egypt. Unfortunately, most were raided by grave-robbers many hundreds or even thousands of years ago, but the tombs still tell us a great deal about the early history of Egypt. Toward the end of the predynastic period, large tombs were built for important people, such as those at Naqada. The largest tombs were lined with bricks and some had paintings on their walls. Eight First Dynasty kings were buried at Abydos, where the burial chamber of the third king, Djer, had a floor made of wooden planks. After Djer, who reigned in about 3040 BC, each royal tomb at Abydos had several chambers containing different grave goods, such as stone vases, copper bowls, gold bracelets, weapons, tools, furniture, and food. At Saqqara, near Memphis, there were elaborate tombs for the princely governors of the delta region.

Above: This stone vessel was carved to look like a basket.

The earliest Egyptian coffins were baskets made from bundles of reeds, as shown here, or simple wooden constructions. The body was placed on its side, with legs bent, just as it had been when burial was directly into the desert sand.

Above: This ivory label shows the fifth king of the First Dynasty, Den. He is striking an Asian enemy, and an inscription reads, "First conquest in the East." The label was attached to a pair of sandals, shown on the other side, among goods in a tomb.

Cylindrical seals were used to show ownership or authority.

A stone statue of Sahure (ruled 2491–77 BC) with a local god of Koptos, a temple and town site on the east bank of the Nile. The second king of the 5th Dynasty, Sahure was buried near Memphis, the Old Kingdom capital.

The Old Kingdom

The Old Kingdom is a name we give to the united Egypt under the rule of four dynasties of kings, beginning around 2686 BC and lasting until 2181 BC. During this 500-year period the kingdom was rich and powerful, with its capital at Memphis. The kingdom was seen as the personal property of the king, and all government was an extension of the royal household. The king's palace was known as the *per-aa* (or "great house"), and later the term was used to refer to the king himself, giving us the word "pharaoh." Egypt was still divided into provinces, under governors selected from noble families. The Old Kingdom was a time of great pyramid-building, at the height of which the Great Pyramid was built. During the 5th and 6th Dynasties, however, the power of kings was weakened when they granted land to their nobles. Then the Nile flood failed for several years, causing famine throughout the land. The Old Kingdom collapsed and was again divided between rival dynasties in Upper and Lower Egypt.

This gold hawk's head, wearing its solid gold crown of plumes, was found at a temple site of Horus. It is a wonderful example of Old Kingdom metalworking.

Pyramid builders

The first Egyptian pyramid was built at the very beginning of the 3rd Dynasty and the Old Kingdom. This was the stepped pyramid built for King Djoser (ruled 2667–49 BC) at Saqqara. The three famous pyramids at Giza (shown right, along with the three smaller queens' pyramids) were built during the 4th Dynasty, as tombs for the kings. Egypt's finest engineers, masons, and sculptors spent years building the pyramids, helped by thousands of workers. The workers were mainly farmers who took time off from their fields, in the belief that if they helped their king with his journey to the afterworld, he would continue to look after them.

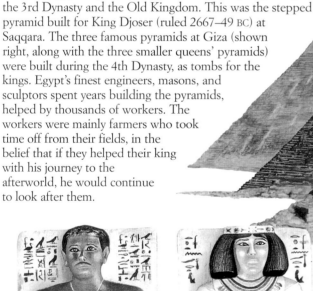

The God Kings

During the rich, successful period of the Old Kingdom, the Egyptians believed that their king was a living god. During his lifetime he was associated with the falcon-headed god, Horus. When a king died, he became associated with Osiris, the father of Horus and god of death and resurrection.

The lateral view of the statue shows King Khafra, also known as Chephren, being protected by the wings of Horus. Horus is perched behind the king's head, stretching his wings out around Khafra's neck, protecting him and lending him supreme power.

Painted statues

These life-size limestone statues date from around 2610 BC. They show Rahotep and his wife Nofret, who were probably the son and daughter-in-law of Snefru, the first king of the 4th Dynasty. Painted statues showed a man's skin as reddish brown and a woman's as pale yellow. Sculpted faces were becoming more lifelike, helped by inlaid eyes of quartz and rock crystal. These were so effective that many tomb robbers removed the eyes first, so that they could not be watched as they went about their business!

Life-sized diorite statue of Khafra (ruled 2558–32 BC), builder of the second pyramid at Giza, seated on his lion throne.

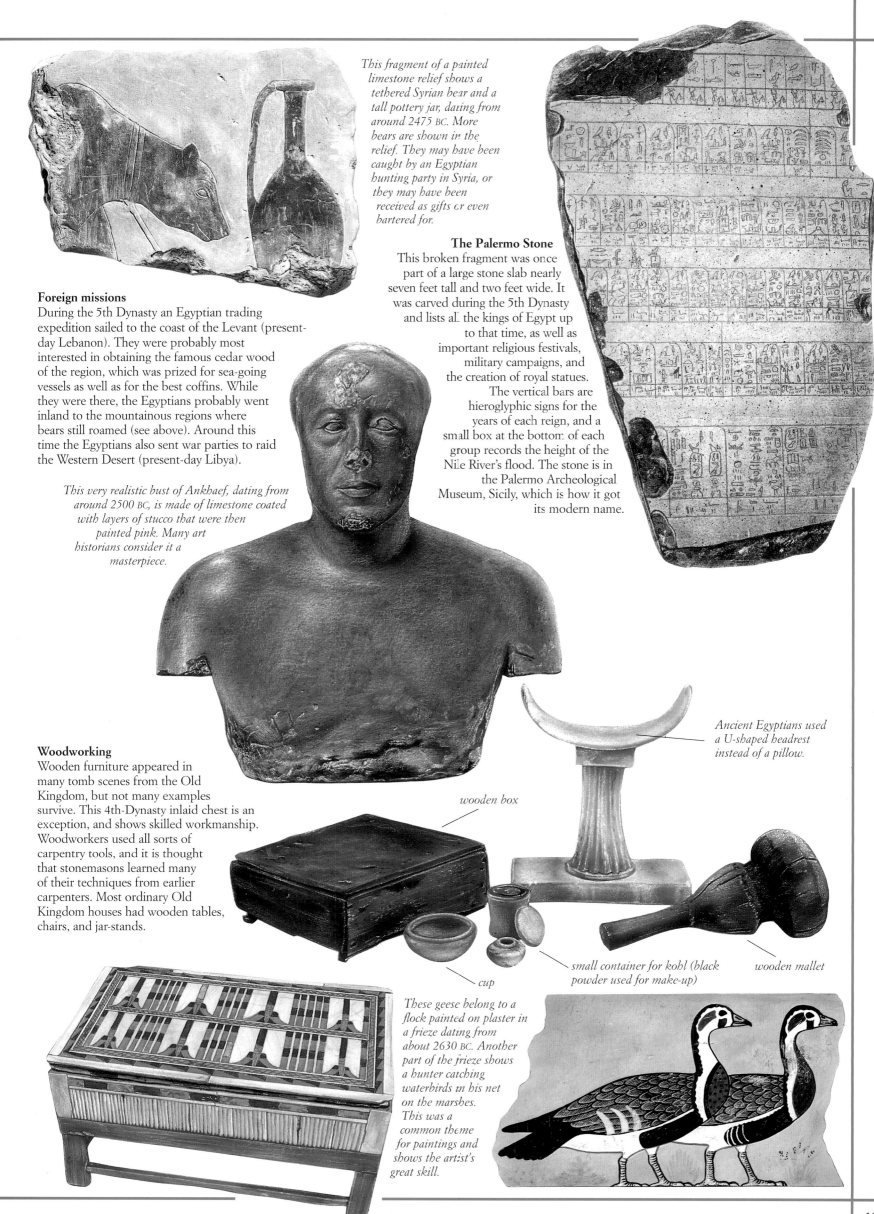

This fragment of a painted limestone relief shows a tethered Syrian bear and a tall pottery jar, dating from around 2475 BC. More bears are shown in the relief. They may have been caught by an Egyptian hunting party in Syria, or they may have been received as gifts or even bartered for.

The Palermo Stone

This broken fragment was once part of a large stone slab nearly seven feet tall and two feet wide. It was carved during the 5th Dynasty and lists all the kings of Egypt up to that time, as well as important religious festivals, military campaigns, and the creation of royal statues. The vertical bars are hieroglyphic signs for the years of each reign, and a small box at the bottom of each group records the height of the Nile River's flood. The stone is in the Palermo Archeological Museum, Sicily, which is how it got its modern name.

Foreign missions

During the 5th Dynasty an Egyptian trading expedition sailed to the coast of the Levant (present-day Lebanon). They were probably most interested in obtaining the famous cedar wood of the region, which was prized for sea-going vessels as well as for the best coffins. While they were there, the Egyptians probably went inland to the mountainous regions where bears still roamed (see above). Around this time the Egyptians also sent war parties to raid the Western Desert (present-day Libya).

This very realistic bust of Ankhaef, dating from around 2500 BC, is made of limestone coated with layers of stucco that were then painted pink. Many art historians consider it a masterpiece.

Woodworking

Wooden furniture appeared in many tomb scenes from the Old Kingdom, but not many examples survive. This 4th-Dynasty inlaid chest is an exception, and shows skilled workmanship. Woodworkers used all sorts of carpentry tools, and it is thought that stonemasons learned many of their techniques from earlier carpenters. Most ordinary Old Kingdom houses had wooden tables, chairs, and jar-stands.

Ancient Egyptians used a U-shaped headrest instead of a pillow.

wooden box

small container for kohl (black powder used for make-up)

wooden mallet

cup

These geese belong to a flock painted on plaster in a frieze dating from about 2630 BC. Another part of the frieze shows a hunter catching waterbirds in his net on the marshes. This was a common theme for paintings and shows the artist's great skill.

The Age of Pyramids

When the Step Pyramid was built at Saqqara around 2660 BC, for the second ruler of the Old Kingdom period, it heralded the beginning of the greatest age of massive monument building in ancient Egypt. Just over a hundred years later, the largest of them all, the Great Pyramid, was built a little farther down the Nile, at Giza. These amazing stone structures were not simply monuments to the dead, however. They were tombs representing the first mound of creation, and they acted as a place where the dead king could be transformed into an eternal spirit and journey to the sky every day. Their mystery has led some to believe that they were also astronomical observatories or giant sundials. By the end of the Old Kingdom period the great age of pyramid building was over, though the tradition was later revived. The last pyramids were built hundreds of years later for Nubian kings in the southern land that the Egyptians called Kush.

This stela shows the seated figure of King Snefru, who was the greatest pyramid builder in Egyptian history. He had two pyramids built at Dahshur – the Bent Pyramid and the Red Pyramid – after his first at Meidum (see below). Snefru was the father of Khufu, for whom the Great Pyramid at Giza was built.

1. Many of the earliest pyramids were built using slanted vertical layers of blocks of stones.
2. By the time of the 4th dynasty much larger blocks were being laid in horizontal layers.
3. Later the pyramids were filled with rough masonry.
4. The last pyramids were filled with mudbricks and had shaped casing stone exteriors.

The pyramid at Meidum was built during the reign of King Snefru (ruled 2613–2589 BC). Today it has a stepped appearance, because it has lost its outer casing. It was in fact the first true, or smooth-sided, pyramid.

The great Step Pyramid built for King Djoser at Saqqara is 200 feet high. It was probably the first monumental stone structure in human history.

Building a pyramid

The large pyramids were tremendous feats of engineering and construction. The Great Pyramid at Giza is made of 2.3 million limestone blocks, each weighing 2.5 tons or more. It probably took about 30,000 men more than 20 years to build. They hauled the blocks into place using ramps, rollers, and wooden sledges, before fitting them tightly together. There may have been a single wide supply ramp at one side of the pyramid, or narrower ramps winding their way around the structure.

Below: The three giant pyramids at Giza. The tallest of them, the Great Pyramid of King Khufu (ruled 2589–66 BC), is 480 feet high and measures 750 feet along each side of its base. It is the oldest of the Seven Wonders of the Ancient World and is the only one still standing today.

Step pyramids

The first pyramid was the stepped structure built by the architect Imhotep for Djoser – the great Step Pyramid. Other 3rd-Dynasty kings also had step pyramids built, before the 4th-Dynasty ruler, Snefru, built the first true pyramid. These step pyramids were formed by a series of rectangular structures set one on top of the other around a core of desert stones, with a burial chamber cut into the rock beneath the pyramid. They were also faced with polished limestone, to give a smooth, gleaming finish, just like the later true pyramids.

The Bent Pyramid at Dahshur, built by Snefru, would have been the highest of them all if its slope had not been changed half way up. The change was probably due to the foundations not being able to support the structure's weight.

Giza

Khufu's Great Pyramid was the first and tallest at Giza. It has two burial chambers within the structure and a third, unfinished chamber below ground. A red granite sarcophagus was found inside the so-called King's Chamber, but the tomb had been robbed in ancient times. The second pyramid was built for King Khafra, son of Khufu, and the third and smallest for Menkaure (ruled 2532–04 BC), Khafra's son. The complex has small "queens' pyramids" which were probably built for the kings' wives, as well as groups of tombs for other members of the royal family and high officials.

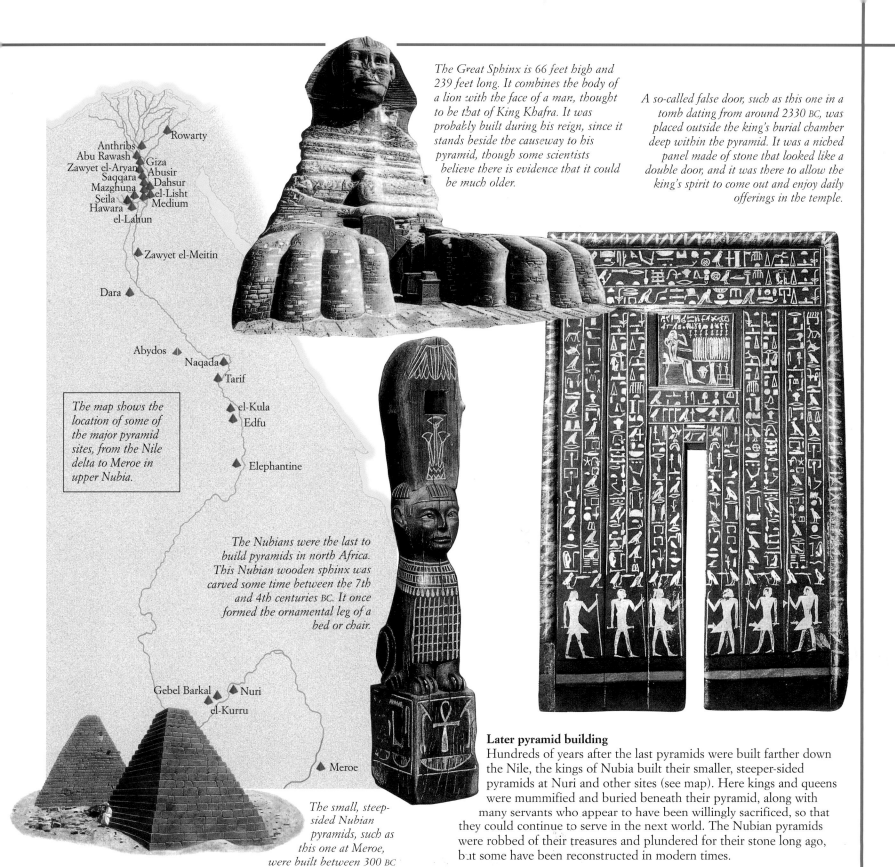

The Great Sphinx is 66 feet high and 239 feet long. It combines the body of a lion with the face of a man, thought to be that of King Khafra. It was probably built during his reign, since it stands beside the causeway to his pyramid, though some scientists believe there is evidence that it could be much older.

A so-called false door, such as this one in a tomb dating from around 2330 BC, was placed outside the king's burial chamber deep within the pyramid. It was a niched panel made of stone that looked like a double door, and it was there to allow the king's spirit to come out and enjoy daily offerings in the temple.

Anthribs
Rowarty
Abu Rawash
Giza
Zawyet el-Aryan
Abusir
Saqqara
Dahsur
Mazghuna
el-Lisht
Seila
Medium
Hawara
el-Lahun

Zawyet el-Meitin

Dara

Abydos
Naqada
Tarif

el-Kula
Edfu

The map shows the location of some of the major pyramid sites, from the Nile delta to Meroe in upper Nubia.

Elephantine

The Nubians were the last to build pyramids in north Africa. This Nubian wooden sphinx was carved some time between the 7th and 4th centuries BC. It once formed the ornamental leg of a bed or chair.

Gebel Barkal
Nuri
el-Kurru

Meroe

Later pyramid building

Hundreds of years after the last pyramids were built farther down the Nile, the kings of Nubia built their smaller, steeper-sided pyramids at Nuri and other sites (see map). Here kings and queens were mummified and buried beneath their pyramid, along with many servants who appear to have been willingly sacrificed, so that they could continue to serve in the next world. The Nubian pyramids were robbed of their treasures and plundered for their stone long ago, but some have been reconstructed in modern times.

The small, steep-sided Nubian pyramids, such as this one at Meroe, were built between 300 BC and AD 350, when Nubia was conquered by the Axumites. Royal burial chambers were situated beneath the pyramids.

It was the duty of priests to look after the pyramid complex. This relief from around 2300 BC shows priests bringing offerings for the deceased.

Pyramid towns

The great pyramid complexes were not isolated monuments. They each had their own town nearby, where priests, officials, and guards lived, along with all those needed to support and supply them. All these people made it possible for the pyramid to function properly as a ritual center. Such towns were probably separate from the less permanent settlements that housed the huge workforces required to build the pyramids. Some craftsmen specialized in this work, while many of the laborers were farmers who joined the workforce during seasons when there was little agricultural work to do.

This reconstruction shows a tomb with a small pyramid in the cemetery at Deir el-Medina, the village built to house artists and craftsmen who worked on the royal tombs in the Valley of the Kings.

Model boats were often placed in tombs, to help the deceased sail to the afterworld. These have helped us learn about the development of Egyptian boats.

Egyptian ship-builders laid down a central board and then added wooden planks, laid edge to edge and lashed together with cords, to build up the hull. The illustration shows how wooden boats were built after about 2600 BC.

In this picture, the Nile is represented by a blue man covered in waves, showing the movement of water. He is holding a palm-rib which is the hieroglyphic sign for "year."

River of Life: the Nile

The river that flowed through their land meant everything to the Ancient Egyptians and their whole way of life was based on it. The calendar year began with the annual flood, which spread rich silt across the land and made it fertile. Without it, they could never have grown plentiful crops in the dry, barren desert. The Egyptians also used the river as the easiest, quickest transport route. They began building boats in predynastic times, first of reeds and then of wood. At first they used paddles, then oars, until they developed a way of harnessing the wind by using sails. These were useful for traveling south, for the prevailing winds blew that way. Traveling north was easy by just drifting downstream with the flow of the river.

The river's course

The Nile is the longest river in the world, measuring 4,145 miles today. It has two main branches, which we call the White Nile and the Blue Nile because of the different colors of their waters. The White Nile begins as the River Kagera in present-day Burundi. It flows into Lake Victoria and then heads north. At Khartoum, the capital of modern Sudan, the river is joined by the fast-flowing Blue Nile. In ancient times it then flowed over a series of six cataracts, or rocky areas of rapids, between Khartoum and Aswan.

Nile boats

All the early Egyptian boats were developed for use on the Nile, and it was only much later that shipbuilders started to think about sea-going vessels. By about 4500 BC predynastic Egyptians were building rafts made of bundles of reeds tied together, which they propelled and steered with paddles. About 1,000 years later, they added a square sail, probably made of woven reeds. By 3000 BC they began to use wood for their ships, probably because they needed stronger vessels to transport massive blocks of limestone to regions where they wanted to build tombs. These wooden boats improved greatly when the Egyptians began importing cedar wood from Lebanon, which was much better than the local acacia.

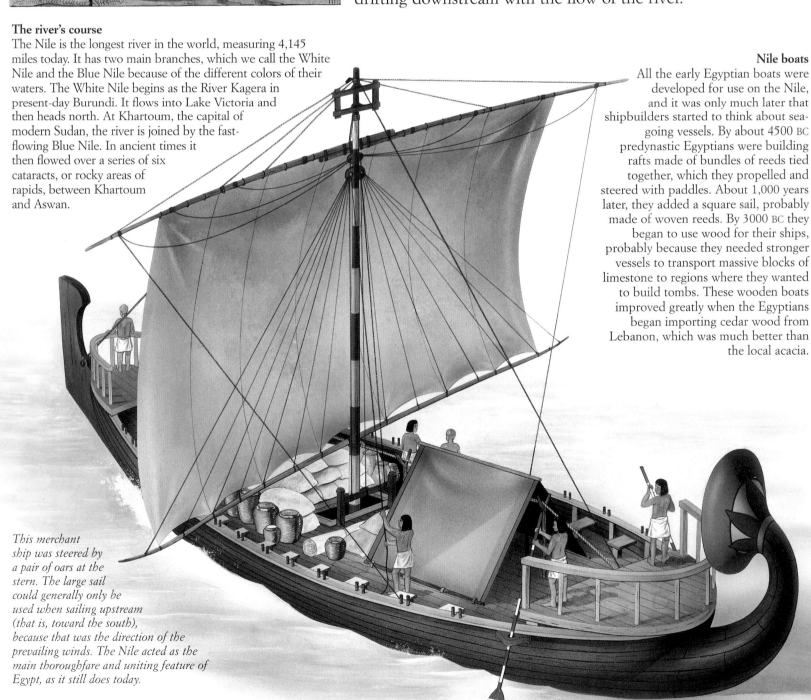

This merchant ship was steered by a pair of oars at the stern. The large sail could generally only be used when sailing upstream (that is, toward the south), because that was the direction of the prevailing winds. The Nile acted as the main thoroughfare and uniting feature of Egypt, as it still does today.

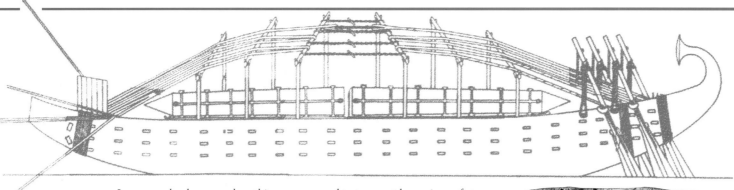

Large wooden barges such as this one were used to transport huge pieces of stone (in this case, two obelisks) from quarries to the appropriate building site.

Three seasons

The Egyptians based their year on the annual cycle of the Nile, dividing it into three seasons of four months each starting from the middle of July. The first season was *akhet*, the time when the river flooded and covered the land with its rich, life-giving silt. Farmers could do nothing with their fields at this time, and many took on work as builders. The second season was *peret*, when the flood waters disappeared and crops were sown. Then, toward the end of a period of drought called *shemu*, the crops were harvested. The ancient seasons show how all-important the Nile was to all Egyptians.

This tile fragment dating from around 1350 BC shows a calf moving playfully among the reeds near the river bank. Wealthy landowners had large herds of cattle.

Bone harpoons from predynastic times. These may have been used to spear fish and hippopotamus.

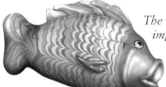

The Nile was an important source of many different kinds of fish.

Inundation

Between June and September each year, heavy rains in the Ethiopian highlands swelled the Blue Nile and another tributary, the Atbara. It was this that caused the Nile to flood. By about the end of September, the floods would begin to subside. But life beside the great river was never easy or predictable, for the flood was never exactly the same two years running, either in its timing or its extent. In order to measure the flood, the Egyptians built series of steps and marks, called Nilometers, at strategic points.

Fishermen using nets and traps to catch fish in the river. Nets may sometimes have been dragged along the river between two boats. Since fish were plentiful, this must have been a very successful method.

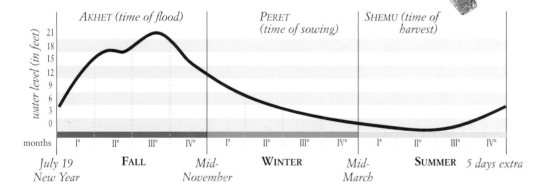

	AKHET (time of flood)	PERET (time of sowing)	SHEMU (time of harvest)

water level (in feet): 21, 18, 15, 12, 9, 6, 3, 0

months: I° II° III° IV° | I° II° III° IV° | I° II° III° IV°

July 19 New Year — **FALL** — Mid-November — **WINTER** — Mid-March — **SUMMER** — 5 days extra

This hieroglyphic calendar shows the year divided into three seasons (see the graph left). The year began on the first day that Sirius, the dog star, reappeared after 70 days during which it was eclipsed by the sun. This was exactly when the annual flood was expected to begin and corresponds to our date of July 19.

The Egyptian calendar

The three seasons, which were based on the annual cycle of the Nile, made up a year that was divided into twelve months, based on observations of the moon. Each month was further divided into three weeks, and each week into ten days. This made a 360-day year, and five extra days were added at the end. These were considered to be holy days on which, according to legend, the gods Osiris, Isis, Horus, Seth, and Nephthys were born. Since the solar year (the time it takes for the earth to travel once around the sun) is actually 365 days and almost 6 hours, and the Egyptians had no leap year, the civil calendar moved one day out of step with the land every four years.

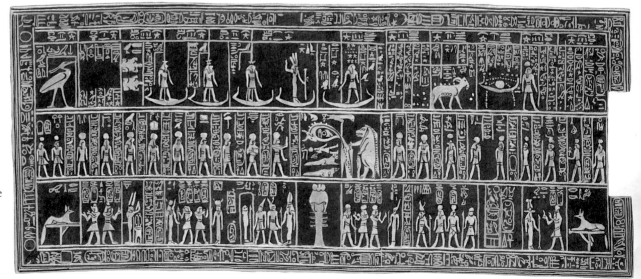

Agriculture and Food

The majority of Egyptians worked on the land, producing enough to feed themselves and their families, as well as to pay taxes in food to the state. The fertile soil around the Nile allowed farmers to grow cereal crops, and these were used to make the two main items of the Egyptian diet – bread and beer. Bread was made at home by housewives or servants, and after about 1600 BC most villages had bakeries. Farmers also kept cattle, goats, and sheep, as well as poultry. Beef was the favorite meat of those who could afford it. Even antelopes and gazelles were bred, but mainly to serve as sacrificial animals. Vegetables and fruit were grown in small plots or gardens, and along with bread these formed the basic diet of poorer people.

Painted wooden model of a farmworker with a digging tool. Vegetables such as onions, garlic, peas, and beans were grown in small square plots.

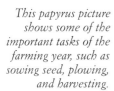

This papyrus picture shows some of the important tasks of the farming year, such as sowing seed, plowing, and harvesting.

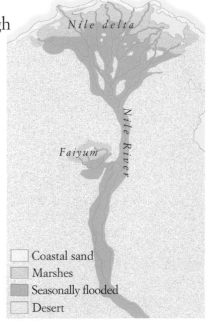

Coastal sand
Marshes
Seasonally flooded
Desert

The map shows the areas that were covered with water each year when the Nile broke its banks during the flood. These were the best farming areas.

Farm animals

Cows were kept for their meat and milk. Cattle were divided by the Egyptians into longhorns and shorthorns, and in the New Kingdom a humpbacked variety was introduced from Asia. Sheep and goats were also reared for their meat, wool, and skin. Pigs were kept, but were perhaps less important since they were regarded as animals of Seth, the god of chaos. Oxen were used for pulling plows, and donkeys for transport. Horses came to Egypt later and were not used in agriculture.

These men are picking grapes in a vineyard. Red grapes grew especially well in the Delta area and the oases because they needed a lot of water. The vines were also fertilized with the droppings of pigeons, which were kept in nearby dovecotes for the purpose.

A young cowherd with his cattle. Cows were the most valuable domestic animals, and every year when the floodwaters subsided, they were driven to fresh pastures where feed had been planted.

Cereal crops

The main cereal crops were barley and a type of wheat called emmer. Two other types of wheat, einkorn and spelt, were also grown. At harvest time in April and May, when the cereals were cut, farmers had an enormous amount of work to do.

After it had been cut with sickles, the grain had to be separated from the chaff by threshing or winnowing (see illustration above), after which the grain was taken to granaries for storage. If the grain had to be taken any great distance, it was transported by boat along the river.

Donkeys were used as pack animals, and also to help with some farm work, such as threshing.

Farmers used simple tools, such as this wooden sickle with a flint cutting edge inserted in it. At harvest time, groups of men went into the fields and cut cereals (left) with such tools.

Beer and wine

Egyptian beer was made from barley, and later also from wheat. It was probably a thick brew, and was very nutritious. A lot of beer was drunk, but it was not as alcoholic as it normally is today. The Egyptians also flavored their alcoholic drinks with spices, honey, and dates. Both red and white wine were made and drunk, though mainly by wealthier people. Wine was stored in pottery vessels, which were sometimes inscribed with the type of wine and its year, like a modern wine label.

This woman is making beer at home, using barley either from special cakes or stale bread. Beer was also made by professional brewers.

These tiny woven baskets were placed as offerings in a tomb. They contain juniper berries and cumin. Herbs and spices were used to flavor beer and food, as well as in purification rituals for the dead. Juniper trees were also used for their wood.

The shaduf

This mechanical tool was made up of a long wooden pole with a bucket-like container hanging from a long rope at one end and a counterbalancing weight, often a large rock or heavy lump of Nile mud, at the other. The pole was mounted on an upright post so that it could swivel around. The shaduf could transfer water from the river or from a canal, and raise it to a higher level at the same time, so it was perfect for irrigating fields and garden plots. It is still used in parts of Egypt today.

Archeologists believe the shaduf was first used in Egypt around 1550 BC, having been introduced probably from Mesopotamia. It was very important in irrigation.

This tomb painting from Thebes dates from about 1240 BC and shows a man using a shaduf to water a garden. The plot was probably used to grow fruit and vegetables.

Fish were sometimes harpooned, as well as being caught in nets or traps. Fish was less expensive than meat and so was particularly popular with less wealthy people. Certain fish were sacred in some areas and were therefore not eaten.

Cooking

Food was cooked in clay ovens in the courtyard, to keep smoke and smells out of the house. Meat was roasted or stewed in pots. Poorer people who had only one room cooked over a fire made in a hole in the floor. During busy farming periods, some women took a cooked meal to their husbands in the fields at midday so that they did not have to stop work. At home, food was served in pottery dishes at low tables, and everyone ate with their fingers. Sticky cakes were made with honey, and fruit such as pomegranates, melons, figs, and dates were plentiful.

These servants are plucking and gutting geese ready for cooking. Geese and ducks (and later, hens) were kept for their meat and eggs, and other wildfowl were hunted in the marshes.

This wooden figure from the Middle Kingdom shows a man fanning a fire to roast a duck.

Butchers at work on an ox. They have tied the animal's back legs together, and the free leg may be cut off to give as a religious offering. Ox meat was the most highly valued, both for eating and for use in temple offerings.

Egyptian Writing

We know from recent discoveries that the ancient Egyptians were already using the script that we call hieroglyphics by around 3250 BC, about 100 years before Egypt was united. The word hieroglyph comes from the Greek for "sacred carving," because the script was used mainly to write inscriptions on temples, tombs, and religious documents. More than 6,000 hieroglyphic signs have been identified, but most of these were introduced in the Late Period. In Old Kingdom times, there were around 750 different signs. The script was used and understood by very few people, however, and from the Early Dynastic period an easier script called hieratic was used for everyday writing. Later, this was replaced by an even simpler script called demotic. After the end of the Egyptian empire, the skill of reading hieroglyphs was lost, and the ancient script was only re-deciphered in 1822. This knowledge has been vital to our understanding of ancient Egypt.

An Egyptian scribe at work. Early scribes used reed brushes and cakes of pigment, which were usually black and red. Later they often used pens cut from the stems of reeds. Scribes wrote on chips of stone, fragments of pottery, leather sheets, and thin wooden boards, as well as on papyrus.

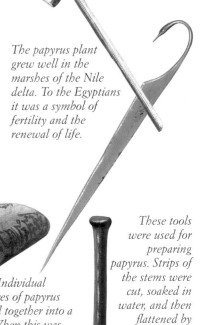

The papyrus plant grew well in the marshes of the Nile delta. To the Egyptians it was a symbol of fertility and the renewal of life.

This ointment vessel, dating from around 2240 BC, bears the hieroglyphic name of King Pepi II. Written characters were thought to be more than just functional: they were living, sacred images, and could even pose a threat to others.

Individual squares of papyrus were fixed together into a roll (above). When this was unrolled, the inside was written on first. The other side was often left blank, and sometimes used later by people who could not afford new papyrus.

These tools were used for preparing papyrus. Strips of the stems were cut, soaked in water, and then flattened by beating. The strips were then laid on top of each other so that they meshed together as they dried.

The three scripts

The first script, hieroglyphics, has three kinds of signs: logograms, or word signs, which show the object they represent (for example, a circle for the sun); phonograms, or sound signs, representing the consonants that make up words (for example, a mouth for the letter "r," a snake for "dj"); and determinatives, signs that help determine the sense of words (for example, the phonograms for the word "wine" might be followed by the sign of a wine jar). Hieratic was a shorter, faster form of writing with joined-up characters developed from hieroglyphics. Demotic was similar, but even quicker to write.

This craftsman's bowl from around 1200 BC has hieroglyphs running around the rim. The inside is decorated with a lotus motif promising immortality.

HIEROGLYPHS	
HIERATIC	
DEMOTIC	

Part of a wooden coffin lid from the 4th century BC. In this late example of hieroglyphics, the columns of inscription are beautifully inlaid in multicolored glass. They show the high standard of craftsmanship that was associated with Egyptian ceremonial writing. The owl stood for the letter "m."

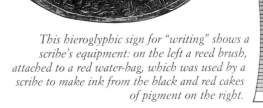

This hieroglyphic sign for "writing" shows a scribe's equipment: on the left a reed brush, attached to a red water-bag, which was used by a scribe to make ink from the black and red cakes of pigment on the right.

Using writing

Only a tiny minority (probably less than 1 percent) of ancient Egyptians could read and write at all. Some historians have suggested that those who understood hieroglyphics were quite happy with this situation, because it restricted knowledge and power to them. In any event, many scribes could only write in hieratic (or later, in demotic), which came to be used for keeping records, writing lists, and for informal letters and notes. Hieroglyphs were usually written from right to left, but could also be written from left to right, or sometimes from top to bottom in columns. Hieratic was always written from right to left.

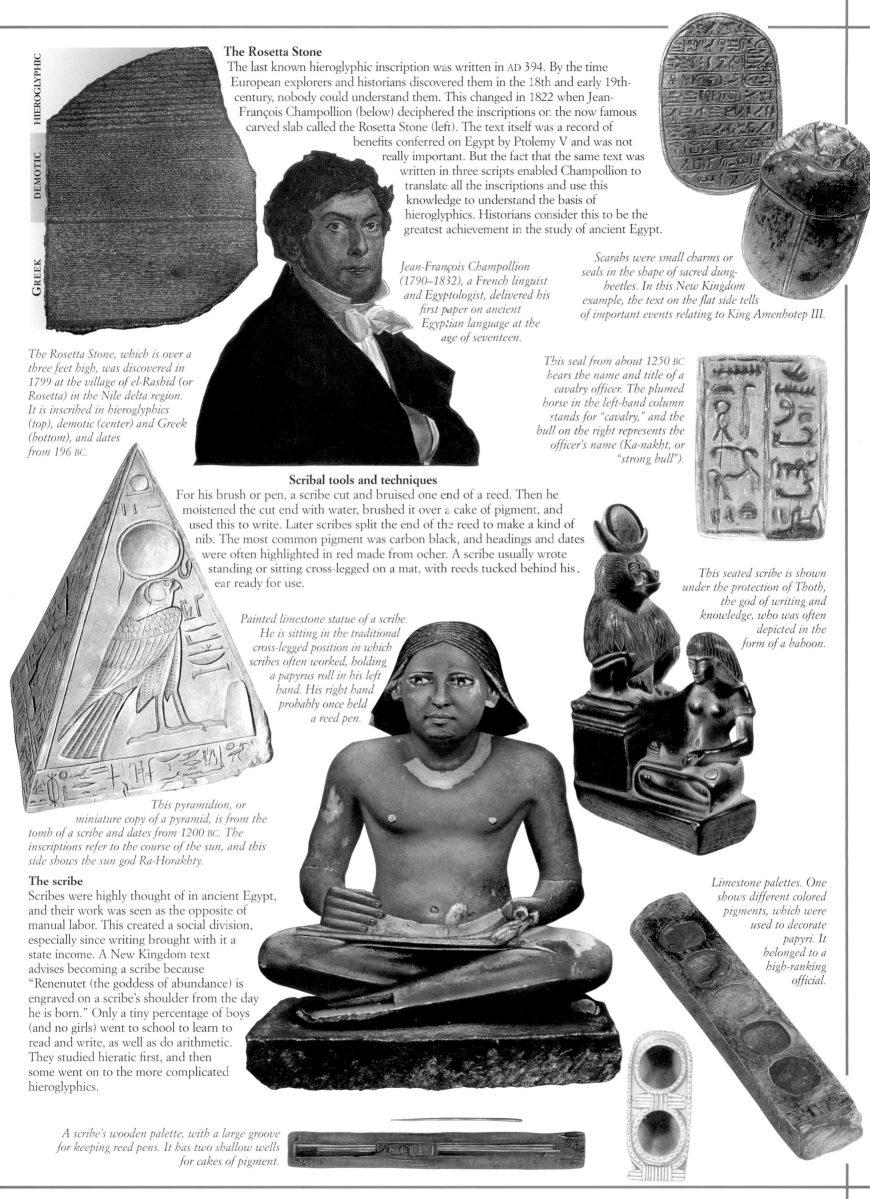

HIEROGLYPHIC

DEMOTIC

GREEK

The Rosetta Stone

The last known hieroglyphic inscription was written in AD 394. By the time European explorers and historians discovered them in the 18th and early 19th-century, nobody could understand them. This changed in 1822 when Jean-François Champollion (below) deciphered the inscriptions on the now famous carved slab called the Rosetta Stone (left). The text itself was a record of benefits conferred on Egypt by Ptolemy V and was not really important. But the fact that the same text was written in three scripts enabled Champollion to translate all the inscriptions and use this knowledge to understand the basis of hieroglyphics. Historians consider this to be the greatest achievement in the study of ancient Egypt.

Jean-François Champollion (1790–1832), a French linguist and Egyptologist, delivered his first paper on ancient Egyptian language at the age of seventeen.

Scarabs were small charms or seals in the shape of sacred dung-beetles. In this New Kingdom example, the text on the flat side tells of important events relating to King Amenhotep III.

The Rosetta Stone, which is over a three feet high, was discovered in 1799 at the village of el-Rashid (or Rosetta) in the Nile delta region. It is inscribed in hieroglyphics (top), demotic (center) and Greek (bottom), and dates from 196 BC.

This seal from about 1250 BC bears the name and title of a cavalry officer. The plumed horse in the left-hand column stands for "cavalry," and the bull on the right represents the officer's name (Ka-nakht, or "strong bull").

Scribal tools and techniques

For his brush or pen, a scribe cut and bruised one end of a reed. Then he moistened the cut end with water, brushed it over a cake of pigment, and used this to write. Later scribes split the end of the reed to make a kind of nib. The most common pigment was carbon black, and headings and dates were often highlighted in red made from ocher. A scribe usually wrote standing or sitting cross-legged on a mat, with reeds tucked behind his ear ready for use.

Painted limestone statue of a scribe. He is sitting in the traditional cross-legged position in which scribes often worked, holding a papyrus roll in his left hand. His right hand probably once held a reed pen.

This seated scribe is shown under the protection of Thoth, the god of writing and knowledge, who was often depicted in the form of a baboon.

This pyramidion, or miniature copy of a pyramid, is from the tomb of a scribe and dates from 1200 BC. The inscriptions refer to the course of the sun, and this side shows the sun god Ra-Horakhty.

The scribe

Scribes were highly thought of in ancient Egypt, and their work was seen as the opposite of manual labor. This created a social division, especially since writing brought with it a state income. A New Kingdom text advises becoming a scribe because "Renenutet (the goddess of abundance) is engraved on a scribe's shoulder from the day he is born." Only a tiny percentage of boys (and no girls) went to school to learn to read and write, as well as do arithmetic. They studied hieratic first, and then some went on to the more complicated hieroglyphics.

Limestone palettes. One shows different colored pigments, which were used to decorate papyri. It belonged to a high-ranking official.

A scribe's wooden palette, with a large groove for keeping reed pens. It has two shallow wells for cakes of pigment.

Wall relief showing Mentuhotep I (ruled 2060–10 BC), wearing the red crown of Lower Egypt, from his cult temple at Thebes. He was the first king to re-unite the two lands and form the first dynasty of the Middle Kingdom.

The Middle Kingdom

After the end of the period that we call the Old Kingdom, there was a period of about 125 years of disunity in Egypt, including a return to conflict between north and south. This conflict was resolved when Mentuhotep I seized the throne of Memphis and assumed control of the whole country, moving the capital to Thebes. This was the beginning of the period that historians call the Middle Kingdom, which lasted from about 2040 to 1782 BC. At this time the Egyptian kings struggled to re-establish power over the country's ruling families, but for a while stability was regained. During the 13th and 14th Dynasties, however, there were many short-reigning rulers and control of Egypt's borders was once again relaxed.

Memphis •

Herakleopolis •

Thinis •

Thebes •

Hierakonpolis •

Controlled by Herakleopolis

Controlled by Thinis

Controlled by Thebes

Controlled by Hierakonpolis

The map shows the most important provinces and their capitals during the First Intermediate Period.

First Intermediate Period
Historians call the time between the Old and Middle Kingdoms the First Intermediate Period, which lasted from 2181 to 2040 BC. During this period was divided between several rulers, some from Herakleopolis, south of Memphis, and others from Thebes. The lack of central government seems to have given the provinces the opportunity to flourish. High-ranking officials chose to be buried near their home towns rather than near their king, which shows how power shifted from the royal court to the local community.

Sphinx statue of King Senusret III (ruled 1874–41 BC), who took power away from provincial governors and placed it in the hands of three regional viziers – one for the north, another for the south, and a third for the island of Elephantine and northern Nubia.

This funerary stela, or stone slab, was carved for a family during the 12th Dynasty (1991–1782 BC). The round top is typical of Middle Kingdom stelae. Large numbers of stelae were erected at sacred sites such as Abydos.

Terracotta model of a Middle Kingdom house. It has an arched doorway and a small window to let in fresh air. The house also has its own drain. A ladder leads up to the flat roof, where Egyptians spent much of their time when the weather was hot. The real house would have been made of mud bricks. The model was placed in a tomb, offering accommodation in the next world.

Painted acacia wood figure of the vizier Nakhti, dating from around 1950 BC. Wood was often still used for funerary statues in the early Middle Kingdom, and this figure also has inlaid eyes. The long proportions of the figure are typical of the period, as is the kilt worn by the vizier.

The role of the king
During the First Intermediate Period rulers were no longer seen as having absolute power, as they had been during the Old Kingdom. The kings of the Middle Kingdom did all they could to strengthen their position and return to a position of unified power, including declaring themselves to be the sons of gods. Powerful families had become used to having much more of a say in the provinces. Regional government was not necessarily weaker or less efficient than central, royal government, but it meant a change of role for the king. Middle Kingdom rulers once again made themselves the central source of authority, and their officials – viziers and district governors – were given the power to represent them throughout the country.

This pectoral, or ornamental breastplate, shows two mirror images of Amenemhet III (ruled 1842–1797 BC) beating a Bedouin with a club. During this period the Arabian nomads of the desert, whom the Egyptians called "sand dwellers" and we know as Bedouin, threatened Egyptian turquoise mines in the Sinai region and were dealt with by force.

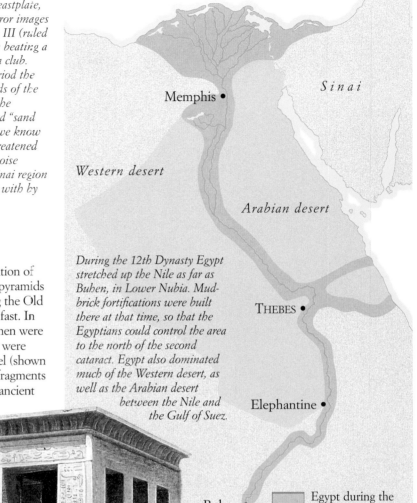

During the 12th Dynasty Egypt stretched up the Nile as far as Buhen, in Lower Nubia. Mud-brick fortifications were built there at that time, so that the Egyptians could control the area to the north of the second cataract. Egypt also dominated much of the Western desert, as well as the Arabian desert between the Nile and the Gulf of Suez.

Egypt during the 12th Dynasty

Area controlled by 12th Dynasty

Architecture

In the Middle Kingdom, kings returned to the tradition of using the pyramid as a royal tomb. But the newer pyramids were smaller and less well constructed than during the Old Kingdom. Perhaps the monuments were built too fast. In this period the best tombs built by wealthy noblemen were cut out of great rock cliffs. The temples at Karnak were extended during this period, and the White Chapel (shown reconstructed, below) of Senusret I was found in fragments at Karnak. It is considered to be a masterpiece of ancient Egyptian architecture and relief sculpture.

This pilaster (a column projecting from a wall) shows Senusret I (ruled 1971–26 BC), who established a garrison at the fortress of Buhen (see map, right). He is holding two ankh amulets, symbolizing life.

A blue faience hedgehog. Animal statuettes were common in Middle Kingdom tombs, but experts are not certain of their purpose. It could be that the hedgehog was supposed to use its protective spines to help the deceased.

New art styles

During the Middle Kingdom period most relief sculpture was painted, so the styles of painting and sculpture were very similar. The faces of human figures were becoming more realistic, replacing the more stylized versions of the Old Kingdom, but bodies were always shown as being young and strong. Huge statues of kings were carved out of granite and other hard stones, and some were so much bigger than life-size that they were placed outside rather than inside temples. The tombs of wealthy nobles were decorated with beautiful painted scenes.

Block statues were introduced in the Middle Kingdom. The original idea of this form of sculpture was probably to present an individual as a guardian to the gateway of a temple. The front of the block was usually inscribed with details about the individual.

This model boat from the First Intermediate Period is typical of wooden models placed in tombs at that time and during the Middle Kingdom. The boat has its single square sail hoisted and is steered by a large oar at the stern.

Control of Nubia

For much of the 12th Dynasty the Egyptians concentrated their military efforts on the southern territory of Nubia. They invaded the Kush region, which was an important source of valuable metals and minerals – gold, copper and gemstones such as amethyst. There were also plenty of cattle and slaves to capture, and the Egyptians knew that Kush led on to farther African lands where they could exchange goods for ebony, ivory, and incense. Seven fortresses were built along the stretch of the Nile's Second Cataract, to protect Egypt and secure trading routes.

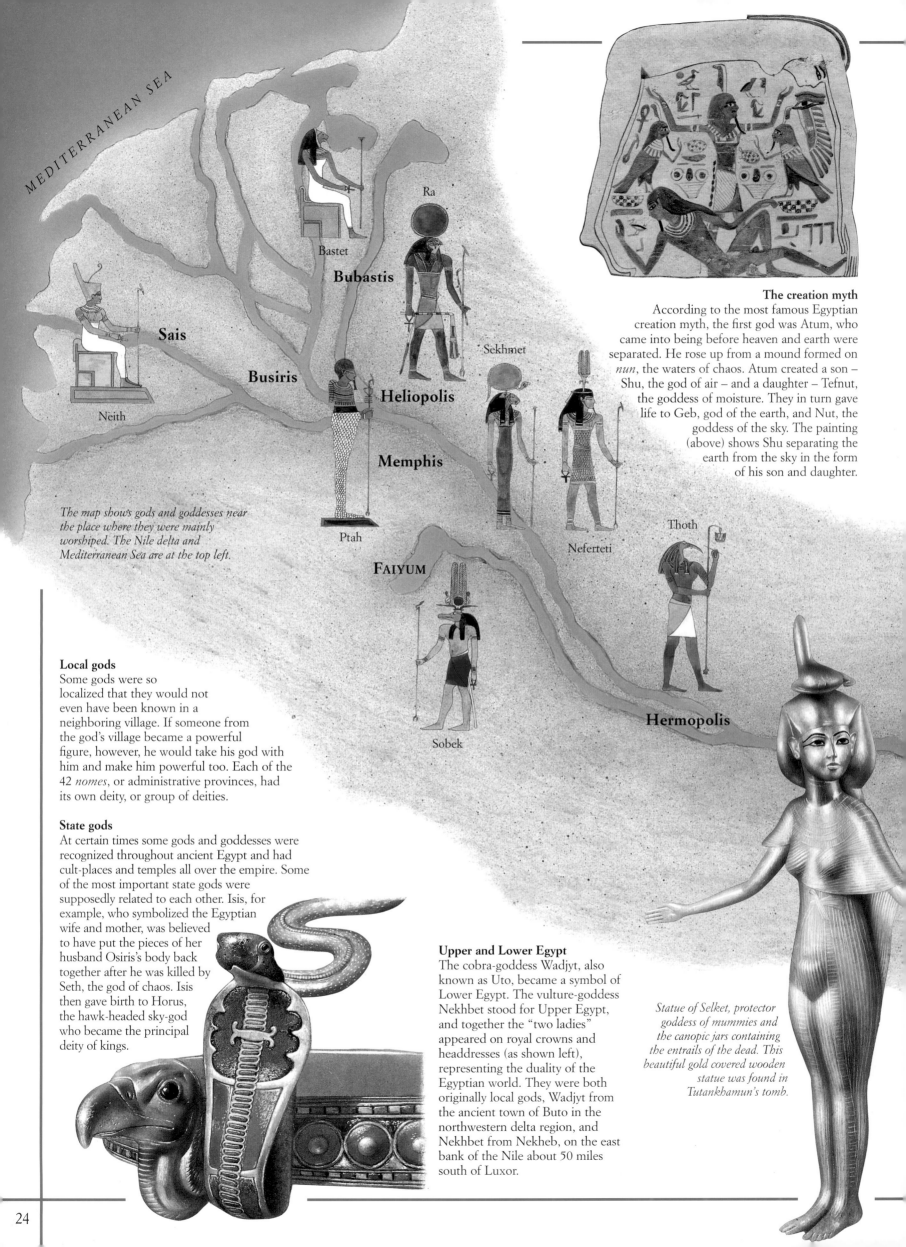

MEDITERRANEAN SEA

Sais

Neith

Busiris

Bastet

Bubastis

Ra

Sekhmet

Heliopolis

Memphis

Ptah

Neferteti

Thoth

FAIYUM

Sobek

Hermopolis

The map shows gods and goddesses near the place where they were mainly worshiped. The Nile delta and Mediterranean Sea are at the top left.

The creation myth

According to the most famous Egyptian creation myth, the first god was Atum, who came into being before heaven and earth were separated. He rose up from a mound formed on *nun*, the waters of chaos. Atum created a son – Shu, the god of air – and a daughter – Tefnut, the goddess of moisture. They in turn gave life to Geb, god of the earth, and Nut, the goddess of the sky. The painting (above) shows Shu separating the earth from the sky in the form of his son and daughter.

Local gods

Some gods were so localized that they would not even have been known in a neighboring village. If someone from the god's village became a powerful figure, however, he would take his god with him and make him powerful too. Each of the 42 *nomes*, or administrative provinces, had its own deity, or group of deities.

State gods

At certain times some gods and goddesses were recognized throughout ancient Egypt and had cult-places and temples all over the empire. Some of the most important state gods were supposedly related to each other. Isis, for example, who symbolized the Egyptian wife and mother, was believed to have put the pieces of her husband Osiris's body back together after he was killed by Seth, the god of chaos. Isis then gave birth to Horus, the hawk-headed sky-god who became the principal deity of kings.

Upper and Lower Egypt

The cobra-goddess Wadjyt, also known as Uto, became a symbol of Lower Egypt. The vulture-goddess Nekhbet stood for Upper Egypt, and together the "two ladies" appeared on royal crowns and headdresses (as shown left), representing the duality of the Egyptian world. They were both originally local gods, Wadjyt from the ancient town of Buto in the northwestern delta region, and Nekhbet from Nekheb, on the east bank of the Nile about 50 miles south of Luxor.

Statue of Selket, protector goddess of mummies and the canopic jars containing the entrails of the dead. This beautiful gold covered wooden statue was found in Tutankhamun's tomb.

A golden statue of Amun, "the hidden one," who in early times was worshiped as a local god in southern Egypt. His cult spread to Thebes, where he became the god of the Theban pharaohs from about 2000 BC onward. At the temple of Karnak he is described as "king of the gods."

Gods and Goddesses

The Egyptians believed that gods and goddesses were involved in the world from the very beginning. According to the best known of their creation myths, a young god first rose from a mound in an ocean of chaos called *nun*. This was the sun-god Atum, and the myth of creation clearly mirrored the most important earthly event in ancient Egypt – the emergence of fertile land after the annual flood of the Nile. According to the myth, Atum created two more deities, and his great-grandchildren were Osiris (the god of death, resurrection, and fertility), Isis (who later gave birth to Horus), Seth (god of chaos and confusion), and the goddess Nephthys. These were major deities, but many more were worshiped in Egypt. Some were local gods, while others spread and became known throughout the land. The gods often appeared as animals, and showed their natural qualities – the strength of a lion (Shu and Tefnut), or the speed and sight of a falcon (Horus). In order to keep the world in balance, the Egyptians honored and worshiped their gods.

Maat, the goddess of truth and justice, represented the harmony and divine order of the universe. She was shown as a kneeling woman with an ostrich feather in her hair, and was often represented simply by the feather itself. The goddess, or her feather, was always present at the judgment of the dead.

This polished slate statue of the goddess Taweret, also known as Thoeris, dates from the 7th century BC. The hippopotamus-goddess was already known during Old Kingdom times, however. She was the guardian goddess of pregnant women and was thought to protect them during childbirth. Her arms and legs are those of a lion, and she supports herself on two looped symbols representing the hieroglyph meaning "protection."

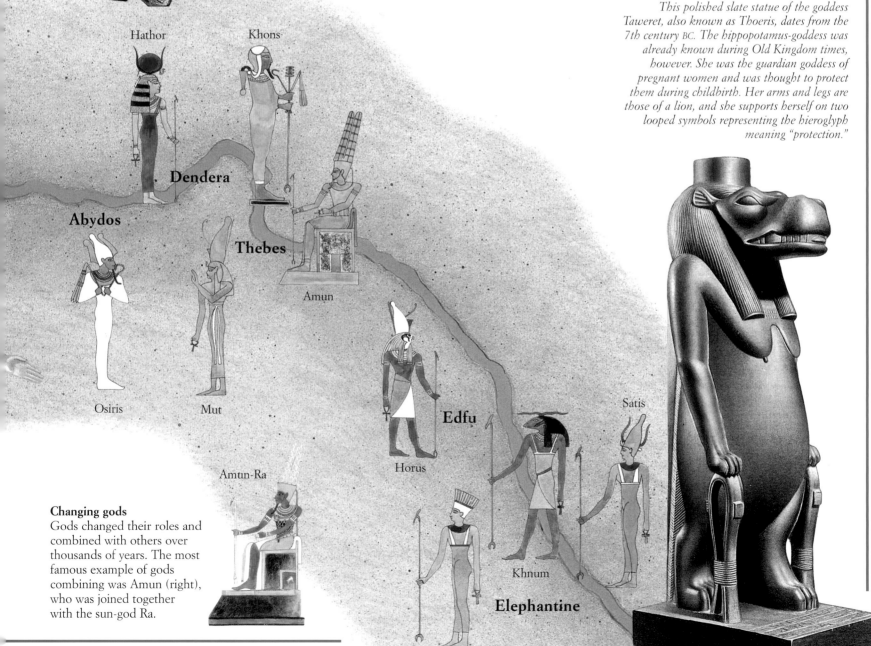

Hathor

Khons

Dendera

Abydos

Thebes

Osiris

Mut

Amun

Horus

Edfu

Satis

Amun-Ra

Changing gods
Gods changed their roles and combined with others over thousands of years. The most famous example of gods combining was Amun (right), who was joined together with the sun-god Ra.

Khnum

Elephantine

Anukis

25

Temples, Priests, and Worship

Each Egyptian temple was dedicated to one of the gods or goddesses. It contained a shrine where the image of the deity was kept in the form of a golden statue. The purpose of the temple was celebration of the cult of the god, but the building did not act as a meeting place for worshipers. The temple's god was served by the chief priest, who was the king of Egypt. Since the king could not attend each temple every day, he was represented by chief priests. Below them were lower levels of priests, who did all the work around the temple. Ordinary people were never allowed in, but they did get the opportunity to see and worship the cult statue on special festival days. Then the priests would take the statue from its shrine and carry it outside the temple walls.

Metal statue of King Tuthmosis IV (1419–1386 BC) kneeling and offering two pots. The Egyptian king was the representative of all mankind and the chief priest of every cult. This meant that in theory only he could care for and make offerings to a god in his temple.

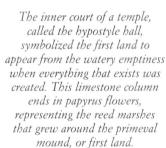

The inner court of a temple, called the hypostyle hall, symbolized the first land to appear from the watery emptiness when everything that exists was created. This limestone column ends in papyrus flowers, representing the reed marshes that grew around the primeval mound, or first land.

A priest's life

Different levels of priests looked after the temple. They washed twice during the day and a further twice during the night. Their heads and bodies were completely shaved, and they wore fine white linen. Their sandals were made of papyrus. There was a great deal of work to do at the temple, in addition to looking after the cult of the local god. Some priests supervised the temple's workshops, while others studied ancient writings in the library of papyrus rolls. There was a lot of organizing to do, running granaries and slaughter-houses for the sacrifices, as well as looking after the land around the temple and teaching future generations of priests. There were also some priestesses (see page 45).

(see page 45).

An offering to the god Amun, who is represented by a ram's head, dating from the 20th dynasty (c.1100 BC). The earliest temples dedicated to Amun were built near Thebes around 2000 BC.

This illustration shows three priests performing a libation for the temple god. The first priest is pouring wine or water onto an incense burner. Note the lotus flower and bread offerings on the ground next to it.

The chief priest

The chief priest of a temple represented the king. He was usually the only one who came into contact with the god to whom the temple was dedicated. His job was to serve the god. Each day before dawn, ritually purified and wearing the purest linen, the chief priest entered the temple carrying offerings of food and drink and chanting prayers. He said to the god, "It is the king who sends me." He removed the clothing wrapped around the statue of the god and cleaned it before putting on layers of fresh linen. Having offered the food and drink, the chief priest left the sanctuary, sealed the door, and swept the floor as he moved away.

This small limestone shrine, just half an inch high, dates from about 1250 BC. Shrines and busts were sometimes kept in people's houses to honor and remember those who had done great service to the local community.

The road to the temple of Luxor was lined with two rows of 365 human-headed sphinxes. The entrance originally had two tall, pointed obelisks, but in 1831 one was removed and put up at the Place de la Concorde, in Paris.

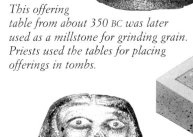

This offering table from about 350 BC was later used as a millstone for grinding grain. Priests used the tables for placing offerings in tombs.

Festivals

Ordinary people only had an opportunity to see the statues of gods that stood inside temples on special festivals. One of the most popular took place each year during the second month of the flood (August/September), and lasted for up to four weeks. The temple of Luxor (above) was specially built for this festival. The statues of Amun and Mut were taken from their temples at Karnak, put inside the cabin of a ceremonial boat, and carried on the shoulders of priests the few miles to the temple of Luxor. The road was packed with people rejoicing at their opportunity to see the gods.

This cutaway illustration shows the layout of a temple. As a priest walked to the sanctuary containing the statue of the god, the floor rose and the walls got closer together, representing the universe at the moment of creation and making the inside of the temple even more mysterious.

FLOORPLAN OF THE TEMPLE OF LUXOR

Building a temple

Like many ancient buildings, Egyptian temples were not built once and then left. They were continually extended and renewed, and new temples were built on top of old. The complex of temples at Karnak, in modern Luxor, was probably started before 2000 BC. Stone was brought from quarries all over Egypt, and most of the structures still standing today were built of huge blocks of sandstone. Mortar was used between blocks. The hypostyle hall of the main temple, dedicated to Amun-Ra, was built by Ramesses II (ruled 1279–12 BC) and has 134 massive columns.

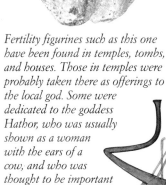

Fertility figurines such as this one have been found in temples, tombs, and houses. Those in temples were probably taken there as offerings to the local god. Some were dedicated to the goddess Hathor, who was usually shown as a woman with the ears of a cow, and who was thought to be important in the destinies of newborn children.

As part of a festival, the statue of the god Khnum is being pulled along in a boat.

Block statue of a priest covered with hieroglyphic inscriptions from the time of the 22nd Dynasty (945–712 BC).

Craftworkers and Artisans

All Egyptian towns and villages had skilled craftworkers who made all the essential everyday things, as well as luxury items such as jewelry. Builders collected mud from beside the Nile, added straw and pebbles, and poured the mixture into wooden frames to make bricks, which were left in the sun to dry. After a house was built of mud-bricks, artisans covered the walls with plaster. Skilled joiners made wooden furniture for the home, and potters and metalworkers made containers and other objects. Most linen was made by full-time weavers, though some women spun their own thread at home. For palaces, temples, and tombs, stonemasons cut and carved limestone, sandstone, and granite. The most skilled craftsmen worked for the royal household, using gold, gemstones, and the finest materials.

This fragment from a New Kingdom fresco shows a carpenter kneeling on scaffolding as he works. He is shaping wood with an adze similar to the one below. The carpenter is shown with unkempt hair and a stubbly beard, which is unusual.

Some of the wide variety of tools used by carpenters. From left to right: a burnisher for smoothing down and polishing; a bronze chisel; a bronze punch with a wooden handle; an adze with a bronze blade bound to the wooden handle with leather.

This gold necklace was found in the tomb of King Psusennes I (ruled 1039–991 BC) at Tanis and has his king names on the oval cartouches. This wonderful piece of jewelry weighs more than thirteen pounds. The finds at Tanis are considered to be second only to those in the tomb of Tutankhamun.

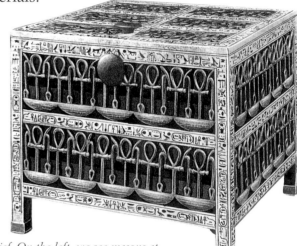

One of the beautiful chests found in the tomb of Tutankhamun. It is made of wood and ivory coated with gold and silver. The main symbols in gold are protective signs and include the ankh, *a T-shape with a loop on top meaning "life." The hieroglyphs around the edge of the chest include the oval-shaped cartouches giving the name of the king.*

Fragment of an 18th-dynasty relief. On the left, we see masons at work, cutting stone and mud bricks. On the right, the vertical section of a house is shown.

Jewelers

From very early times the Egyptians used gold, lapis lazuli, turquoise, and amethyst in pieces of jewelry. By the time of the Middle Kingdom, jewelers were producing work of great elegance, much of which has survived because it was buried with the owners in tombs. Craftsmen used bow drills to pierce beads and other jewels, and they inlaid jewels into wood, metal, and glass paste. Thin sheets of gold were easy to work, and were used to cover wooden statues and other objects. Many jewelers must have been employed in the king's palaces and to work on his tomb, as well as in temple workshops. Poorer people also wore simple jewelry made from less valuable gemstones or glazed ceramic materials.

Woodworkers

From the Early Dynastic period Ancient Egyptian artisans used copper tools for woodwork. Timber from many different trees was used: the sycamore fig for coffins, tables, and chests; ash for bows and other weapons; acacia for boat-building; and cedar imported from Lebanon for ships and the best coffins. Carpenters pulled long saws through timber to cut it into planks, which they shaped with adzes. They used mallets and chisels to cut joints, and bradawls and bow drills to make holes. Furniture for the home mainly consisted of tables, chairs, stools, and jar-stands. Woodworkers showed great technical skill in building two-wheeled chariots, which were introduced by the Hyksos invaders around 1700 BC. They also carved large solid statues and small models as tomb offerings.

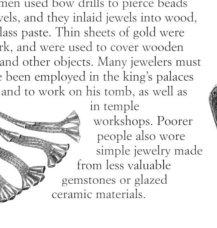

These gold sandals come from the tomb of King Sheshonq II (c.890 BC). They were an important element of the tomb offerings since it was believed that they would allow the king to walk in the afterlife.

Mastery of metal

The first metal to be used in Egypt was copper, which was mined in the desert to the east of the Nile, as well as to the south in Nubia. From the Middle Kingdom period, tin was added to copper to make bronze, which was harder and stronger. The metals were melted over charcoal-burning furnaces and then poured into pottery molds. Final shaping was done by hammering when the metal had cooled. Some iron was imported, but it was probably not smelted in Egypt until the 6th century BC. Goldsmiths usually beat their precious metal into shape, or it was melted and cast in molds. They also used a method called granulation, by which granules of gold were stuck to an object by soldering.

This painted earthenware vase dates from the Ptolemaic period (305–30 BC). It is decorated with floral designs in relief.

This highly decorated bronze situla is much later than the one above. It was used by priests to sprinkle holy water during special ceremonies, and the base was tapered to allow it to rest on a stand.

This ceramic vessel was made on a simple wheel around 1400 BC. Its tall, long-necked shape and style of painting are typical of the New Kingdom period, when pottery became more decorative than it had been during earlier dynasties. The vase also has the sacred wedjat eye of Horus painted on.

The owners probably used this elegant bronze water basin and tall jug for washing their hands before a meal. They date from around 1400 BC.

Pottery

Mud and silt from the Nile River were used to make clay for pots, which were shaped by the potter, polished with a pebble to give a burnished red appearance, and then fired in a kiln. This kind of pottery is known as "Nile silt ware," and another kind, which used different clay from Upper Egypt, is called 'marl clay ware." Potters made storage jars, cooking pots and serving vessels, using a wheel that they had to spin with one hand while they shaped the clay with the other. After about 500 BC Egyptian potters had use of a foot-operated wheel, which allowed them to make vessels much more quickly. Styles of painting pottery, or whether pots were decorated at all, changed throughout the dynasties and periods.

A fragment of millefiori glasswork, with its characteristic flower patterns. Thin rods of different-colored glass were put into a hot mass of glass and fused together to make bands of color.

Textiles

Almost all Egyptian clothes were made of linen, which itself was made from the flax plant. Flax was harvested by pulling it out of the ground, a back-breaking job mainly done by men. The stems were then soaked to make them soft, beaten, and finally combed to separate the fibers. Women spinners then twisted the fibers on a spindle to make thread. The thread was woven into linen on a loom, which was a simple wooden frame pegged to the ground. Most Egyptian clothes were made of plain white linen. Some pieces of wool have been found, but experts believe that there may have been a religious taboo against its use. Cotton and silk were only introduced in Roman times.

Part of an ornamental funerary pectoral, or breastplate, from the Ptolemaic Period. It is made of glass paste encrusted with gold and silver.

Flax and linen

Stems and fibers of the flax plant are shown (above) in three different stages of preparation for making linen. A spinner used the wooden spindle to twist the fibers into a strong thread ready for weaving. The pieces of linen with colored borders come from the New Kingdom period. Linen clothes needed constant laundering, and by New Kingdom times there were professional launderers in Egyptian villages. The ancient Egyptians took a great deal of trouble to make sure that their clothes were clean and neat.

Glassmaking

The art of glassmaking was probably first introduced into Egypt in the 15th century BC, and the Egyptians seem to have regarded glass almost as a precious stone. It was made by heating quartz, sand, and natron in clay crucibles, adding some copper to produce green and blue glass. The molten mass was then poured into a mold or rolled out into thin rods. Vessels were also made by dipping a core of mud and sand into molten glass. Plain and colored glass were also used as inlays in metal jewelry and other materials. The technique of glass-blowing was only developed during the 1st century BC.

Painted limestone bust of Nefertiti (ruled c.1350–34 BC), who was the principal wife of King Akhenaten. She was a very powerful woman, but later in her husband's reign she seems to have disappeared. Akhenaten was succeeded as king by a mysterious person called Smenkhkara, and some experts believe this may have been Nefertiti.

Horus, the falcon god of the sky, was celebrated from the time of the first dynasties as the main god of kingship.

Kings and Queens

The king of Egypt, whom we also call the pharaoh, was an absolute ruler with total power over his people. The Egyptians believed that he was a living god, representing Horus, the god of the skies, and through him ensuring that their world was well-balanced, successful, and prosperous. They thought that without this divine power of the king, there would be chaos. The king was also chief priest, looking after and celebrating all the gods, though he delegated this authority to other priests. At the same time he was the earthly ruler and military leader. We call the king's wife "queen," but to the Egyptians she was the "great royal wife." Most kings had several wives. The king's mother (or "queen mother") was next in importance, and a few women ruled Egypt themselves as pharaoh.

The king's main duty
Egyptian kings believed that their main role and duty was to fight the forces of chaos and make sure that the delicate balance of life was maintained. This would ensure the continued existence and success of the whole world as the Egyptians knew it. The balance that the king had to maintain was represented by the goddess Maat, who was the favorite daughter of the creator god and wife of the god of wisdom. Once the world was created, Maat lived among humans on earth and was looked after by the king, who was like a brother to her.

King Amenhotep I (ruled 1525–04 BC), in his royal role of chief priest, making an offering. The king's name means "Amun is content," referring to the deity who is called "king of the gods" at the temple of Karnak.

This gilded silver statuette of a 13th-century-BC king is offering a figure of the goddess Maat to a god. The king is doing his duty in making sure that the world functions properly during his reign.

Ramesses II (ruled 1279–13 BC), known as "the Great," was a famous military leader who led his armies into the Middle East. He fought a defensive battle against the Hittites, and later married two of their princesses. His principal wife was Nefertari.

Symbols of kingship

Among the many symbols of kingship were the various crowns, especially the double crown that combined the rule of Upper and Lower Egypt. These were enhanced by the vulture and cobra of the two lands, as well as the scepter, false beard, and striped headcloth (called a *nemes*) that can be seen on Tutankhamun's famous gold mask. Two other items depicted a king: a crook, which was a symbol of government; and a flail, which was associated with the gods Osiris and Min.

White crown
Plume of Osiris
Royal beard
Scepter
Crook
Flail

The cross shape with a loop on top was the hieroglyphic sign for "life." The dog-headed scepter on top of this amulet represented prosperity, and the amulet belonged to a king. It showed that he had been granted eternal life by the gods.

Queen Hatshepsut (ruled 1498–83 BC) was the daughter of King Tuthmosis I and Queen Ahmose Nefertari, and she married her half-brother Tuthmosis II.

This picture shows the god Osiris sitting on a throne as a king of Egypt. He is wearing many of the royal regalia, or symbols of kingship. Most high-ranking Egyptians were clean-shaven, but since gods were often shown wearing plaited beards, kings wore a false beard to show their status as living gods.

A female "king"

When King Tuthmosis II died, his daughter by his principal wife – Hatshepsut –was not heir to the throne. This honor went to Tuthmosis's son by another, less important wife. But since Tuthmosis III was very young, Hatshepsut was appointed regent and it was she who took all the important decisions. She then had herself crowned "king" and effectively ruled Egypt in place of her stepson. She was supported by the priests of the god Amun. During her reign she organized building work at Thebes, sent trading expeditions to Punt and Sinai, and ordered military campaigns. Some of her monuments show her in a king's costume and wearing a royal beard.

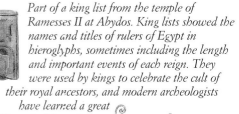

Part of a king list from the temple of Ramesses II at Abydos. King lists showed the names and titles of rulers of Egypt in hieroglyphs, sometimes including the length and important events of each reign. They were used by kings to celebrate the cult of their royal ancestors, and modern archeologists have learned a great deal from them.

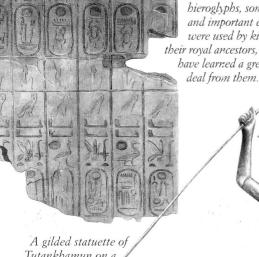

A gilded statuette of Tutankhamun on a raft, wearing the red crown of Lower Egypt, and about to spear Seth, the god of chaos, who took the form of a hippopotamus.

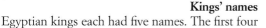

The goddesses Wadjyt (left) and Nekhbet (right), this time in human form instead of being represented by a cobra and vulture, put the double crown on King Ptolemy VIII's head.

Kings' names

Egyptian kings each had five names. The first four were given when a king took the throne. The first was "Horus," which was written inside a panel representing the royal palace; the god was now in the palace (*per-aa* in Egyptian, which led to our word pharaoh). The second name was "He of the two ladies," referring to the cobra and vulture goddesses. The third was "Horus the gold," which probably referred to the sunlit sky. The fourth was "He of the sedge and the bee," which referred to Upper and Lower Egypt. The last name was the king's "birth name" – the name we use – which was introduced with the words "son of Ra" (the sun god).

This carving shows King Akhenaten (ruled 1350–34 BC) and Queen Nefertiti with three of their six daughters. They are seen receiving the rays of the sun-god Aten, whose cult they worshiped in place of Amun. This was considered by many to be wrong, and the king and queen's names and faces were later scratched off some lists and artifacts.

The New Kingdom

After the end of the Middle Kingdom period, Egypt was ruled for about a hundred years by a people called the Hyksos. When they were finally driven out in 1570 BC, a new period began, which we call the New Kingdom. Three dynasties of Egyptian kings ruled through this period, which lasted until 1069 BC. One of the earliest New Kingdom rulers, Tuthmosis I, was the first to have a tomb cut into the rocks of the Valley of the Kings. During his reign, and later, Egypt expanded its empire into the Middle East, as well as south into Nubia. The control of Palestinian trade and desert goldmines brought more wealth to Egypt, where temple-building continued and spread to Nubia. Later kings had to defend Egypt against the Hittites, Sea Peoples, and Libyans, and the New Kingdom empire gradually weakened.

Limestone figure of the first New Kingdom king, Ahmose I (ruled 1570–46 BC), who finally drove the Hyksos from the delta region. Ahmose began a great imperial age for Egypt by invading Canaan to the north and Nubia to the south.

Second Intermediate Period

The hundred years between the end of the Middle Kingdom and the beginning of the New Kingdom is called the Second Intermediate Period (1792–1570 BC). During this period a confederation of Nubian chiefs overthrew Egyptian rule and ran their Kingdom of Kush from Kerma (see the map, left). The delta region of Lower Egypt was taken over by Asiatics called the Hyksos, who migrated into the region and ruled it from their new capital at Avaris. The Hyksos may also have had an alliance with the Kushites in the south.

Founding the New Kingdom

During the Second Intermediate Period the 17th Dynasty of Egyptian kings continued to rule from Thebes. The dynasty's last two rulers, Seqenenre Tao II and Kamose, campaigned against the Hyksos, until they were finally driven out by 1570 BC. Kamose's younger brother Ahmose became the first king of the 18th Dynasty and founded the New Kingdom. Ahmose reorganized national and local government, rewarding local princes who had helped the Theban cause against the Hyksos with important positions. A new imperial age had begun.

This relief shows men from Punt, on the East African coast, bearing gifts to the trading expedition sent by Queen Hatshepsut. Punt (probably modern Somalia or Ethiopia) was a source of many exotic products.

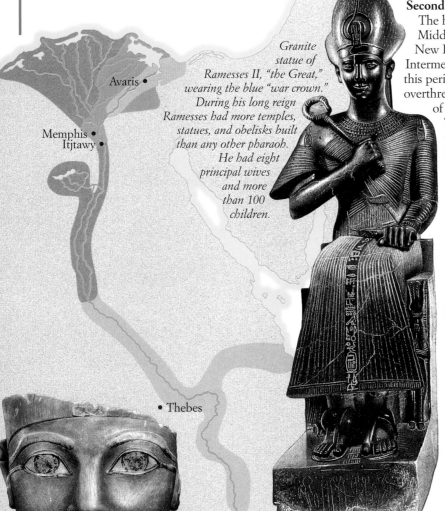

Granite statue of Ramesses II, "the Great," wearing the blue "war crown." During his long reign Ramesses had more temples, statues, and obelisks built than any other pharaoh. He had eight principal wives and more than 100 children.

- Avaris
- Memphis
- Itjtawy
- Thebes
- Kerma

Colossal head of Queen Hatshepsut.

14th Dynasty
16th Dynasty
Kingdom of Avaris
Disputed area
Kingdom of Thebes
Kingdom of Kush

The map shows how Egypt splintered into many kingdoms during the Second Intermediate Period.

The Hyksos capital of Avaris developed into a large city. At the beginning of the New Kingdom, the Egyptians rebuilt the citadel, giving it a thick mud-brick wall and adding a palatial fortress (shown in the reconstruction, right).

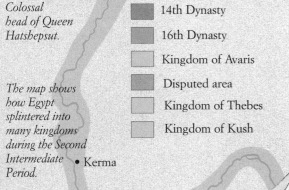

This fragment is one of thousands found at Avaris that made up wall paintings. Since they are clearly Minoan in origin, they suggest that King Ahmose may have made an alliance with the great Mediterranean power on the island of Crete. The paintings may once have decorated the walls of the royal citadel built on the site of the earlier Hyksos capital.

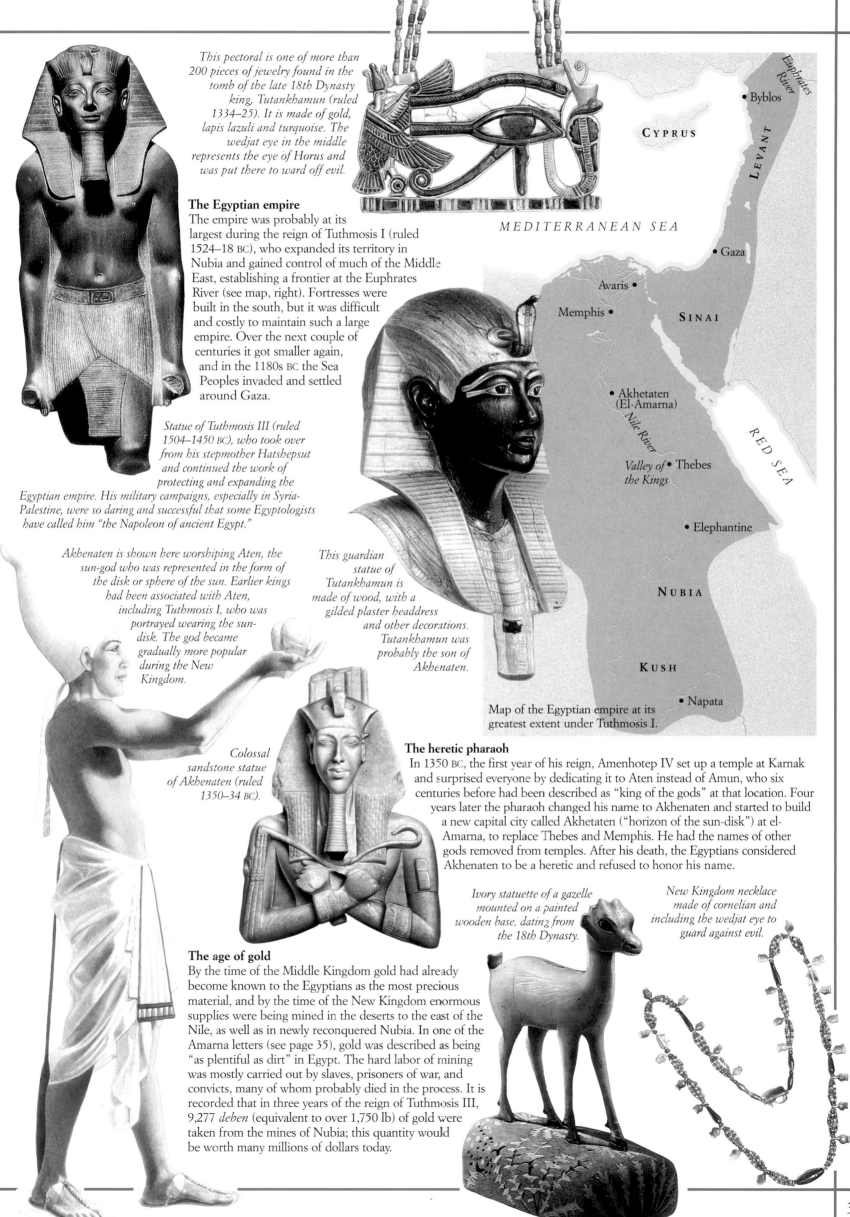

This pectoral is one of more than 200 pieces of jewelry found in the tomb of the late 18th Dynasty king, Tutankhamun (ruled 1334–25). It is made of gold, lapis lazuli and turquoise. The wedjat eye in the middle represents the eye of Horus and was put there to ward off evil.

The Egyptian empire

The empire was probably at its largest during the reign of Tuthmosis I (ruled 1524–18 BC), who expanded its territory in Nubia and gained control of much of the Middle East, establishing a frontier at the Euphrates River (see map, right). Fortresses were built in the south, but it was difficult and costly to maintain such a large empire. Over the next couple of centuries it got smaller again, and in the 1180s BC the Sea Peoples invaded and settled around Gaza.

Statue of Tuthmosis III (ruled 1504–1450 BC), who took over from his stepmother Hatshepsut and continued the work of protecting and expanding the Egyptian empire. His military campaigns, especially in Syria-Palestine, were so daring and successful that some Egyptologists have called him "the Napoleon of ancient Egypt."

Akhenaten is shown here worshiping Aten, the sun-god who was represented in the form of the disk or sphere of the sun. Earlier kings had been associated with Aten, including Tuthmosis I, who was portrayed wearing the sun-disk. The god became gradually more popular during the New Kingdom.

This guardian statue of Tutankhamun is made of wood, with a gilded plaster headdress and other decorations. Tutankhamun was probably the son of Akhenaten.

Map of the Egyptian empire at its greatest extent under Tuthmosis I.

CYPRUS

MEDITERRANEAN SEA

Euphrates River

LEVANT

Byblos

Gaza

Avaris

Memphis

SINAI

Akhetaten (El-Amarna)

Nile River

RED SEA

Valley of the Kings • Thebes

Elephantine

NUBIA

KUSH

Napata

Colossal sandstone statue of Akhenaten (ruled 1350–34 BC).

The heretic pharaoh

In 1350 BC, the first year of his reign, Amenhotep IV set up a temple at Karnak and surprised everyone by dedicating it to Aten instead of Amun, who six centuries before had been described as "king of the gods" at that location. Four years later the pharaoh changed his name to Akhenaten and started to build a new capital city called Akhetaten ("horizon of the sun-disk") at el-Amarna, to replace Thebes and Memphis. He had the names of other gods removed from temples. After his death, the Egyptians considered Akhenaten to be a heretic and refused to honor his name.

Ivory statuette of a gazelle mounted on a painted wooden base, dating from the 18th Dynasty.

New Kingdom necklace made of cornelian and including the wedjat eye to guard against evil.

The age of gold

By the time of the Middle Kingdom gold had already become known to the Egyptians as the most precious material, and by the time of the New Kingdom enormous supplies were being mined in the deserts to the east of the Nile, as well as in newly reconquered Nubia. In one of the Amarna letters (see page 35), gold was described as being "as plentiful as dirt" in Egypt. The hard labor of mining was mostly carried out by slaves, prisoners of war, and convicts, many of whom probably died in the process. It is recorded that in three years of the reign of Tuthmosis III, 9,277 *deben* (equivalent to over 1,750 lb) of gold were taken from the mines of Nubia; this quantity would be worth many millions of dollars today.

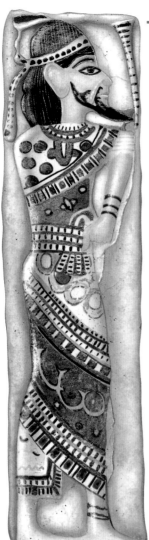

Egypt and its Neighbors

With deserts to the west and east, and the Mediterranean Sea to the north, Egypt was naturally protected from many of its neighbors. Trading missions led the Egyptians north to Syria and west to Libya, where frictions also caused the occasional war. In the Sinai region to the east, the Bedouin nomads also had to be kept under control, for they constantly attacked Egyptian turquoise mines. To the south was Nubia. This region was an important source of gold, copper, and gemstones. There were also plenty of cattle and slaves to capture, and the Egyptians knew that Nubia led on to farther African lands where they could exchange goods for ebony, ivory, and incense. For hundreds of years there were raids between the two kingdoms, and the Nubians adopted some of the religion, art, and customs of the Egyptians, including building pyramids.

Captive Bedouin. As well as attacking the turquoise mines in Sinai the Bedouin invaded parts of the Nile delta region.

Captive Syrian. In 1176 BC, during the reign of Ramesses III, the Egyptian navy destroyed the Sea Peoples' fleet off the Syrian coast. At the same time the Egyptians defeated the rest of their army in Syria.

Captive Libyan. Many Libyans were brought to Egypt after their defeat in 1179 BC. Their enforced settlement led to them becoming a powerful group and later coming to power as the 22nd and 23rd Dynasties.

Captive Hittite. The Hittites fought Egypt for control of Syria (see opposite).

Captive Nubian. At various times in their history, the Egyptians controlled Nubia and Kush, to the south of their empire.

The enemies of Egypt

The five pictures of foreign captives (above and right) are all tile inlays from the mortuary temple of Ramesses III (ruled 1182–51 BC) at Medinet Habu. The walls of the temple are also decorated with scenes from the pharaoh's various campaigns, especially his wars against the Libyans and the Sea Peoples, and show him smiting his enemies.

The Middle East

Egyptian rule in Canaan was marked by alternating periods of war and peace. During the peaceful times international trade prospered all over the eastern Mediterranean. Ugarit, a port in northern Syria, became a major center of commerce. There was a two-way flow of goods between Egypt and Canaan. A coalition of local peoples, including the Mitanni, was decisively beaten by the army of Tuthmosis III at the Battle of Megiddo in about 1470 BC. The coastal town of Byblos, in modern Lebanon, was also important to the Egyptians and is mentioned on the Amarna tablets (see opposite).

This fragment of a wall painting from around 1400 BC shows a Canaanite offering food, gold, and horses to the Egyptian pharaoh. This may have been Amenhotep II, who undertook three military campaigns in Syria and the Middle East.

A Hittite king or god.

This reconstructed wall painting comes from the 19th-century BC tomb of Khnumhotep III at Beni Hassan on the east bank of the Nile. It shows a group of Semitic nomads, probably from Canaan, trading with Egyptians. The amount of luggage and the presence of women and children suggest that the nomads wanted to settle in Egypt. The Egyptians are shown with red skins.

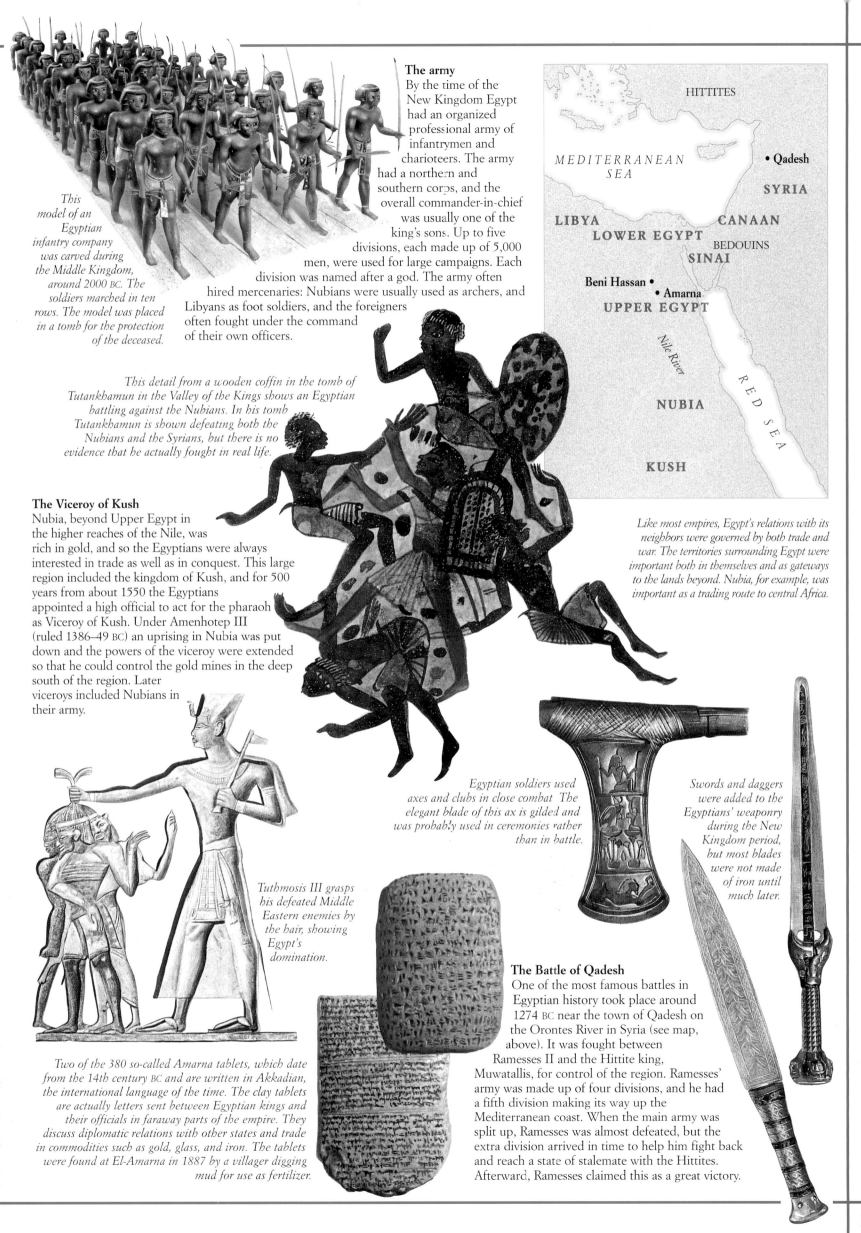

The army

By the time of the New Kingdom Egypt had an organized professional army of infantrymen and charioteers. The army had a northern and southern corps, and the overall commander-in-chief was usually one of the king's sons. Up to five divisions, each made up of 5,000 men, were used for large campaigns. Each division was named after a god. The army often hired mercenaries: Nubians were usually used as archers, and Libyans as foot soldiers, and the foreigners often fought under the command of their own officers.

This model of an Egyptian infantry company was carved during the Middle Kingdom, around 2000 BC. The soldiers marched in ten rows. The model was placed in a tomb for the protection of the deceased.

This detail from a wooden coffin in the tomb of Tutankhamun in the Valley of the Kings shows an Egyptian battling against the Nubians. In his tomb Tutankhamun is shown defeating both the Nubians and the Syrians, but there is no evidence that he actually fought in real life.

The Viceroy of Kush

Nubia, beyond Upper Egypt in the higher reaches of the Nile, was rich in gold, and so the Egyptians were always interested in trade as well as in conquest. This large region included the kingdom of Kush, and for 500 years from about 1550 the Egyptians appointed a high official to act for the pharaoh as Viceroy of Kush. Under Amenhotep III (ruled 1386–49 BC) an uprising in Nubia was put down and the powers of the viceroy were extended so that he could control the gold mines in the deep south of the region. Later viceroys included Nubians in their army.

Like most empires, Egypt's relations with its neighbors were governed by both trade and war. The territories surrounding Egypt were important both in themselves and as gateways to the lands beyond. Nubia, for example, was important as a trading route to central Africa.

Egyptian soldiers used axes and clubs in close combat. The elegant blade of this ax is gilded and was probably used in ceremonies rather than in battle.

Swords and daggers were added to the Egyptians' weaponry during the New Kingdom period, but most blades were not made of iron until much later.

Tuthmosis III grasps his defeated Middle Eastern enemies by the hair, showing Egypt's domination.

Two of the 380 so-called Amarna tablets, which date from the 14th century BC and are written in Akkadian, the international language of the time. The clay tablets are actually letters sent between Egyptian kings and their officials in faraway parts of the empire. They discuss diplomatic relations with other states and trade in commodities such as gold, glass, and iron. The tablets were found at El-Amarna in 1887 by a villager digging mud for use as fertilizer.

The Battle of Qadesh

One of the most famous battles in Egyptian history took place around 1274 BC near the town of Qadesh on the Orontes River in Syria (see map, above). It was fought between Ramesses II and the Hittite king, Muwatallis, for control of the region. Ramesses' army was made up of four divisions, and he had a fifth division making its way up the Mediterranean coast. When the main army was split up, Ramesses was almost defeated, but the extra division arrived in time to help him fight back and reach a state of stalemate with the Hittites. Afterward, Ramesses claimed this as a great victory.

This painted wooden model, found in a tomb dating from about 1990 BC, shows cattle being counted for tax purposes. Officials and scribes sit in a pavilion, along with the tomb-owner. In front of them, a herdsman is being beaten, probably for trying to forge the count.

Administering Egypt

Since the king of Egypt was an absolute ruler, in theory he was totally responsible for running the entire empire. In reality this was impossible, and the king had a hierarchy of officials to carry out his wishes and deal with all the necessary administration. The vizier, or chief minister, was the top official, and he was backed up by a range of regional governors who ran all the separate *nomes*, or provinces, into which Egypt had been divided almost from the very beginning. The most important task of all these officials was to raise taxes, in the form of surplus grain and goods, which went toward supporting the royal family, the officials themselves, priests and scribes, as well as the army. The officials also found workers to help with major state projects such as pyramid-building.

This fragment of a wall painting, dating from around 1400 BC, shows how officials tried to prevent fraud. A land surveyor is using string knotted at regular intervals to measure the size of fields of ripe grain. This was done before the harvest in order to check that the amount of grain later declared for tax purposes was correct.

This wooden statue, carved around 2490 BC, shows a priestly official named Ka-aper. He officiated in a temple institution called the House of Life, training priests in the reading of sacred texts and teaching children to become scribes.

Model of a granary from around 2000 BC. Large amounts of people's taxes were paid in grain, which was sent to such granaries under the authority and protection of high-ranking officials. Most of the state granaries were near temples and royal buildings.

Taxes

The collection of taxes was central to the government of ancient Egypt. The tax was generally levied on farming produce, and officials and scribes were sent out to measure fields and count numbers of livestock, from herds of cattle to flocks of geese. Since money did not exist before the Late Period, taxes were paid in kind, often in amounts of grain. This was stored in state granaries (see right). Other products such as gold ingots, linen, reed mats and even honey were also used as payment, and these were forwarded to special state treasuries and storehouses.

This stela (above) marks the level of the Nile flood in 1831 BC. The line through the oval at the bottom shows the height of the flood waters. Annual taxes were calculated according to the amount of land that was watered and fertilized by the flood.

When a farmer's grain had been harvested, it was put into jars and measured in hekats; 16 hekats made a khar, or sackful. The results were carefully recorded by scribes and used to calculate taxes.

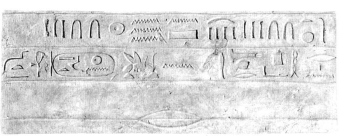

Laws

The king was the supreme law-maker and judge, but in practice, he delegated these powers to his high-ranking officials. During the New Kingdom there was a council of judges called a *kenbet*, often made up of regional governors and priests. Egyptian law was based on the concept of *maat* (correct behavior representing the divine order of the universe), which meant that its basis was a common-sense view of right and wrong. Punishment could be harsh: suspects were often beaten with sticks, and tomb robbers were sentenced to death. In some villages, workers had their own *kenbet* to rule on matters such as theft, unpaid work, or wife-beating.

Two of three Syrian princesses who were part of the royal harem of Tuthmosis III. The princesses were probably presented to the king by a Syrian ruler in order to seal a peace treaty, and in Egypt they were all given the title of "king's wife."

The vizier

The vizier, or chief minister, was the state's highest official. He served as the king's representative in all areas of government apart from religious and military affairs. He was usually given a number of titles, such as "chief of all the king's works" and "royal chancellor." The vizier directed the running of the country, including regional authorities, and he was responsible for the treasuries and storehouses that were vital to Egypt's economy. During the New Kingdom overall authority was divided and there were separate viziers for Upper and Lower Egypt.

Ramose, vizier under Tuthmosis III, receiving a ritual purification. He is wearing the official clothing of a vizier, a calf-length apron that was held by a strap around the neck. His staff and scepter show that he holds a high social position.

Below: painting of the hall of the vizier Rekhmire around 1430 BC. The vizier himself originally appeared in the painting, but he was later removed. His officials are seen receiving others. Also shown is the vizier's messenger, who took his orders around the land.

The king's wives

By the time of the New Kingdom, when the Egyptian Empire expanded, peace treaties were usually sealed by the marriage of the pharaoh to a princess of the foreign land that had been involved in war or dispute. During the 18th Dynasty princesses were presented by the Syrians (see above), and later by the Mitanni of western Asia to Tuthmosis IV. These diplomatic marriages were partly made to counter the threat from the Hittites. A little over 100 years later, a daughter of the Hittite king became one of the many wives of Ramesses II.

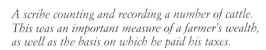

A scribe counting and recording a number of cattle. This was an important measure of a farmer's wealth, as well as the basis on which he paid his taxes.

A Middle Kingdom scribe carved in ivory. He is sitting in the typical scribe's pose, with his papyrus on his knees. The hieroglyphs on the papyrus record the scribe's profession and family tree.

King Menkaure, builder of the third pyramid at Giza, is shown in this statue flanked (on his right) by the goddess Hathor, and (on his left) by the local deity representing the 17th nome of Upper Egypt. The local deity wears the emblem of her province on her head.

Local administration

From very early times Egypt was divided into administrative districts called *nomes*. The names for the *nomes* were almost always derived from the names of the local gods and goddesses. Besides collecting taxes, administrators were responsible for finding laborers for large state works projects, such as building a pyramid or temple. At a local level, some of the larger temples had their own administration and were not obliged to pay taxes or provide labor.

Trade

The source of Egypt's agricultural wealth and very existence – the Nile River – was also its main trade route, connecting the lower lands of the delta with the upper lands of Nubia. From early times Egyptian traders also traveled by sea beyond their borders, along the Mediterranean coast to the west to Libya, to the northeast to Canaan and the Middle East, and down the Red Sea to a land called Punt. Land routes were mainly across desert, and the Egyptians built forts along them to protect their caravans from attack. Their grain and linen were exchanged for goods such as cedar wood and ivory, using systems of barter and diplomatic exchange. There was no money in Egypt before about 400 BC, but there was a scale of value based on weights of copper. Above all, Egypt had plenty of what everyone else wanted – gold.

A gold coin that was minted around 350 BC, probably in Memphis. One side of the coin has a hieroglyphic inscription that reads "fine gold." The reverse shows a prancing horse.

These slaves have their arms and legs bound. Foreign slaves became more common in Egypt as trade increased and the empire expanded. Most slaves were prisoners of war. Some were owned by communities rather than individuals, and they may have helped to increase the production of goods for further trade.

The Egyptians made fine linen for trade. This linen tunic, which was worn like a shirt, was found in a tomb dating from about 1400 BC. It is a specially fine tunic with braid trimming around the neck and hem.

An official of the royal treasury weighs gold rings on a pair of scales, using weights for measurement. The results were then recorded on papyrus rolls. Careful records were kept of everything stored in the treasury, including materials and finished goods.

Gold mummy mask of King Psusennes I (ruled 1039–991 BC), with inlaid work of lapis lazuli and glass. Gold was plentiful in Nubia, which was a major reason why the Egyptians constantly traded and warred with their southern neighbors.

Weights and measures

A knowledge of weights and measures was important to Egyptian trade. Since there were no coins before the Late Period, weights were used to express the value of things. These used the basic unit of a weight of copper called a *deben*. We know from some lists of property that a goat was valued at 1 *deben*, while a bed was worth 2.5 *deben*, but these values probably fluctuated. As the basic unit of measurement, the royal cubit was measured by rods (see right) or by lengths of knotted string. The volume of liquids and materials such as grain was measured in special containers.

A gilded wooden cubit-rod from about 1370 BC. The royal cubit (almost 21 inches), based on the length of a man's forearm, was the main unit of linear measurement. It was made up of 7 palm widths, each of which comprised 4 thumb-width digits, making 28 digits to the cubit.

Africa

Nubia was an important source of gold, copper, and amethyst, as well as cattle and slaves. It was also the route by which goods such as ebony and ivory were brought to Egypt. The Egyptians went on trading expeditions to the land of Punt, in East Africa, which may have been modern Somalia or Ethiopia. They brought back myrrh and other fragrant herbs and spices, leopard skins, and live animals such as baboons and dogs. An inscription in Queen Hatshepsut's temple describes such an expedition: "Never was the like brought back to any ruler since the world began."

Ivory inlaid into wooden furniture, from the royal tombs at Kerma, capital of the kingdom of Kush. From about 2500 to 1500 BC the Kushites controlled the major trade routes in Nubia that linked Egypt with the rest of Africa.

Trade routes

Within Egypt itself, the main trade route was the Nile River. Since their narrow fertile land was surrounded by desert, caravan routes were very important to the Egyptians. Archeologists are finding more evidence that the Egyptians had a system of routes which they controlled and guarded, including major caravan stops, to allow their traders and travelers safe passage. They even built watchtowers. The route to Punt took traders and explorers across the eastern desert to the Red Sea, from where they sailed down the East African coast.

Goods exchanged

The Egyptians mainly exported agricultural produce (mostly in the form of grain), papyrus and linen, as well as gold. They imported cedar wood from Lebanon, which they used for boat-building and to make coffins. Ebony wood and ivory from elephant tusks were brought from Africa to use especially as furniture decoration. Incense, myrrh, and oils came from East Africa and Arabia, for use in perfumes and cosmetics. Iron was later imported to make strong tools and weapons.

This model of an Egyptian servant carrying a vessel is made of painted wood and ivory and dates from 1350 BC. The vessel is a faithful replica of the type of container that was imported from Syria at that time.

This gold and silver New Kingdom vase, with its handle in the form of a goat, shows Asian influences in its style, including the fabulous griffins engraved on the wide neck. It was during this period that the Egyptian empire was at its largest and contacts abroad were at their greatest.

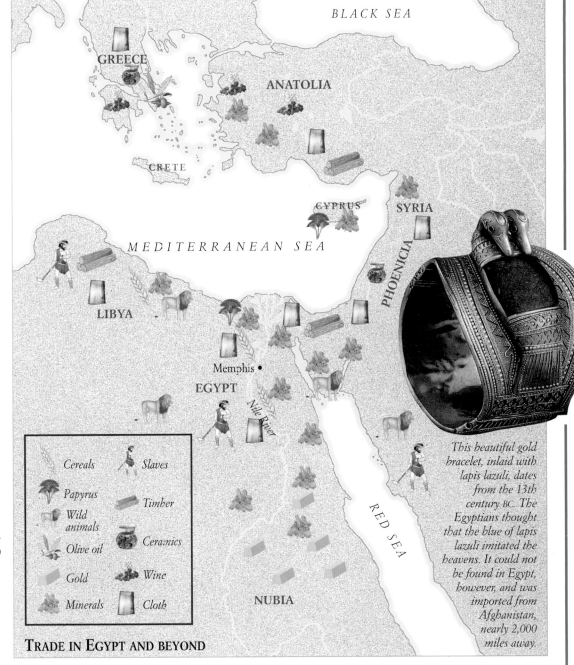

TRADE IN EGYPT AND BEYOND

Cereals
Papyrus
Wild animals
Olive oil
Gold
Minerals
Slaves
Timber
Ceramics
Wine
Cloth

This beautiful gold bracelet, inlaid with lapis lazuli, dates from the 13th century BC. The Egyptians thought that the blue of lapis lazuli imitated the heavens. It could not be found in Egypt, however, and was imported from Afghanistan, nearly 2,000 miles away.

This wall painting from around 1450 BC shows some of the African products prized and imported by the Egyptians: leopards, baboons, ebony, ivory, and ostrich eggs.

Barter

Most trade, both within Egypt and beyond, was carried out by bartering – exchanging goods of equal value. Individual items were valued in terms of numbers of copper *deben* and were exchanged accordingly. When dealing with foreigners, such as people from the land of Punt, the Egyptians seem to have simply offered goods in exchange for what they wanted. With the Middle Eastern states, however, high-value goods were often exchanged by way of diplomatic gifts. Foreign rulers sent gifts to Egypt, for example, and asked for gold statues in return.

The Middle East

The Egyptians were already trading by sea with the Mediterranean coast of Syria in the Early Dynastic Period. Imported wood was used in the royal tombs at Abydos, and a 2nd-Dynasty Egyptian vase was discovered at the Lebanese port of Byblos. Trade with Byblos continued to flourish throughout the Old Kingdom period, and this may have included the exchange of lapis lazuli from Afghanistan. During the New Kingdom the situation was changed by the rise of the Hittites, and control of Middle East trade was interrupted by war.

Metal weights, such as this one in the shape of a rabbit, were made in units of debens (which were made up of 10 kite).

This alabaster container was used to measure liquids and dates from New Kingdom times. The stone weights were used in the same way as metal weights; lighter ones were made of pottery.

Egyptian Art

Most of the earliest pieces of Egyptian art that have survived for modern archeologists to study were carved in stone. One of the earliest royal sculptures is an almost life-size seated statue of King Djoser, from around 2650 BC. Relief sculpture, or wall carving, decorated the walls of temples and tombs in the Old Kingdom. Much less painting has survived from the earlier dynastic periods, not surprisingly, but it had a similar design to the carvings. Outlines were drawn first, and then filled in with even, flat colors. There are so many paintings in Theban tombs and at other sites dating from the New Kingdom period that it is often called the "golden age" of Egyptian painting. Though overall styles did not change dramatically over thousands of years, individual techniques improved and became more complex.

Profile of a human face in bright blue glass. The eyes were made using colored stone. It dates from New Kingdom times.

The granite statue of Hatshepsut (below) dates from about 1460 BC and is from her mortuary temple at Deir el-Bahri. She is wearing the royal false beard and is shown in sacrificial pose, holding a ritual water vessel.

Beautiful terracotta figure of a dancing woman from the predynastic period – about 4000–3500 BC. Finds at Naqada and other sites from the same period have also revealed pieces of pottery and ivory combs.

Faience shabti figurine dating from about 1350 BC. These inscribed figurines, usually made in the shape of a mummy, were placed in tombs to help the deceased in the afterlife. They developed during the Middle Kingdom period.

Early wall paintings

The amazing works found in Painted Tomb 100 at Hierakonpolis (left) are the earliest wall paintings found in Egypt. They date from around 3300 BC. They were discovered in 1898 by archeologists James Quibell and Frederick Green, who opened more than 200 predynastic graves at the site. But the rock-cut Tomb 100 was outstanding. Its walls were lined with mud bricks, and in one chamber the surfaces had been smoothed and the paintings applied. Unfortunately the location of the tomb was not clearly noted, and it was lost again beneath the drifting sands.

Wall paintings in a tomb at the ancient city of Hierakonpolis. The large scene shows river-going ships, painted in white with dark-colored cabins. The smaller one is a detail showing animals and people.

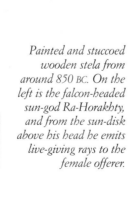

Painted and stuccoed wooden stela from around 850 BC. On the left is the falcon-headed sun-god Ra-Horakhty, and from the sun-disk above his head he emits live-giving rays to the female offerer.

Papyrus and lotus

Both plants feature heavily in Egyptian art throughout the ages. The papyrus was the heraldic plant of the delta region and Lower Egypt, which it represents to the left of the sun-god in the painted stela (right). Since it grew from the Nile mud, the papyrus was thought of as flourishing on the primeval mound of creation. For this reason it was used as decoration on columns in temple courts (see page 26). The lotus, or water lily, represented Upper Egypt, and in creation myths the sun rose out of a lotus floating on the original ocean of chaos. The lotus appears on the right of the stela.

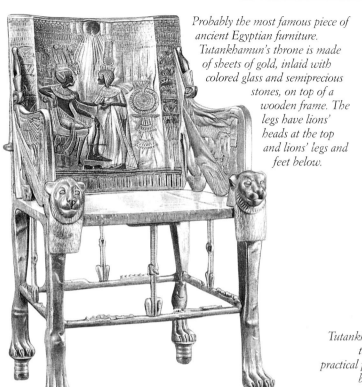

Probably the most famous piece of ancient Egyptian furniture. Tutankhamun's throne is made of sheets of gold, inlaid with colored glass and semiprecious stones, on top of a wooden frame. The legs have lions' heads at the top and lions' legs and feet below.

Magnificent mask

Tutankhamun's death mask is probably the best-known work of art in the whole of Egyptian history. It was made from two sheets of gold, which were joined together by hammering. The gold is inlaid with carnelian, lapis lazuli, and colored glass. The whole mask weighs about 20 lb, and on the back is the inscription of a spell asking the gods to protect each of the king's facial features. The mask is a portrait of the king's face, and its purpose was to help the *ba* spirit recognize the body. The magnificence of the piece and its beautiful detail made it a work of art that has lasted more than 3,000 years.

Tutankhamun's death mask was found covering the face of the king's mummy. It served a practical purpose, for the face was found to be the best-preserved part of the king's mummy.

Materials

Egyptian artists were perfectly at ease working in a wide variety of materials. Tutankhamun's throne (above) is a good example. As well as gold, the artist used silver sheet, colored glass, faience and semiprecious stones to create the detailed picture of the king and queen beneath the rays of the sun-disk, symbol of the god Aten. For the king's kilt alone, nearly 500 tiny pieces of various materials were used, each one cut and positioned with absolute precision.

Detail of the figures of Tutankhamun and his wife Ankhesenamun, from the back of the throne (above). The king sits in a relaxed pose, while the queen holds an ointment container in her left hand.

Paints and colors

From the beginning of the dynastic period, most painting in tombs and elsewhere was done on plastered surfaces. First the surface was divided into a grid of squares, onto which craftsmen drew an outline of the picture. Painters then colored in, before the draftsmen restored the outlines, usually in dark brown or black. Yellow, red, and brown colors came from a mineral called ocher. White came from lime and was also mixed with other colors to lighten them. Blue was made by grinding a copper substance to powder, and black pigment was usually made from soot.

Below: this ornamental pectoral, or breastplate, is made of gold, with inset semiprecious stones. It was found in Tutankhamun's tomb. The wedjat eye at the top was put there to ward off evil. Once again lotus and papyrus plants are depicted.

Wooden models of servants were placed in tombs to help the deceased in the afterlife. This painted wooden model, dating from around 2270 BC, shows a man with his hands in an earthenware vessel of fermenting beer. Models of men and women grinding grain and making bread were also common.

This humorous ink drawing appears on a fragment of limestone dating from the 12th century BC. It shows a cat wielding a large stick to herd a flock of ducks.

Detail of a wall painting from a Theban tomb, dating from around 1100 BC. The picture shows a wild-looking cat, representing the sun-god Ra, killing the snake-god of the underworld, Apophis. The action takes place in front of a sacred tree.

Anonymous artists

In ancient Egypt most art served a religious purpose. Because of this it was essential that the subject of a work of art, whether a god, king, or other important figure, could be identified by name. The name of an artist very rarely appeared. Artists usually worked in teams, when for example they were decorating a tomb, and so it was important that they did not show an unusually distinctive style. Despite this, most ancient Egyptian art is lively and inspired, suggesting that its creators were happy to remain anonymous.

Daily Life

Most ordinary Egyptian men and women lived with their families in houses made of sun-dried mud bricks. These were mostly quite bare, with a few stools and low tables. Wealthier families had larger houses, with guest rooms and a beautiful garden. Styles of clothing and hair did not change much over the centuries. Most adults spent most of the day working – the men in the fields and the women at home – but there were plenty of games and entertainment. Adults played a board game called *senet*, and children had all sorts of toys and pets. Music was a popular form of entertainment, and wealthy people sometimes hired professional musicians. People also prayed at home to gods such as the merry dwarf-god Bes, and they kept statues of some of the gods in their houses.

Leather was stitched together with papyrus twine to make sandals, though reed sandals were more common.

Many adults had their hair completely shaved off, but those that had hair looked after it carefully. Heavy wigs were common, especially for women, and combs such as this were used for real and artificial hair.

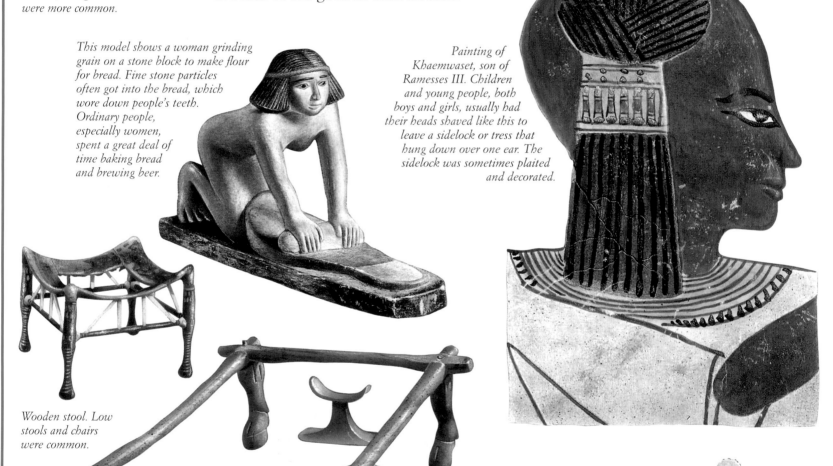

This model shows a woman grinding grain on a stone block to make flour for bread. Fine stone particles often got into the bread, which wore down people's teeth. Ordinary people, especially women, spent a great deal of time baking bread and brewing beer.

Painting of Khaemwaset, son of Ramesses III. Children and young people, both boys and girls, usually had their heads shaved like this to leave a sidelock or tress that hung down over one ear. The sidelock was sometimes plaited and decorated.

Wooden stool. Low stools and chairs were common.

Furniture
Most ordinary people's houses had little furniture, and most was made of wood. One of the best Egyptian woods was sycamore fig, which was used to make tables and chests (as well as coffins). Low tables were used, and low chairs and stools (see above) went with these. Wooden boxes and chests served for storage. Beds had wooden legs to raise them off the floor, which along with wooden headrests were used to try to keep away crawling insects. A range of furniture was found in the tomb of an architect called Kha who lived in the workmen's village near the Valley of the Kings, and much of our knowledge comes from this.

Wooden bed frame with headrest, blanket, and slippers. Beds had mattresses made from rushes, and the headrest served instead of a pillow.

Music was a very popular form of entertainment, and a wide range of instruments were played. Some women worked as professional musicians, providing entertainment for others. This woman is playing an early form of lyre.

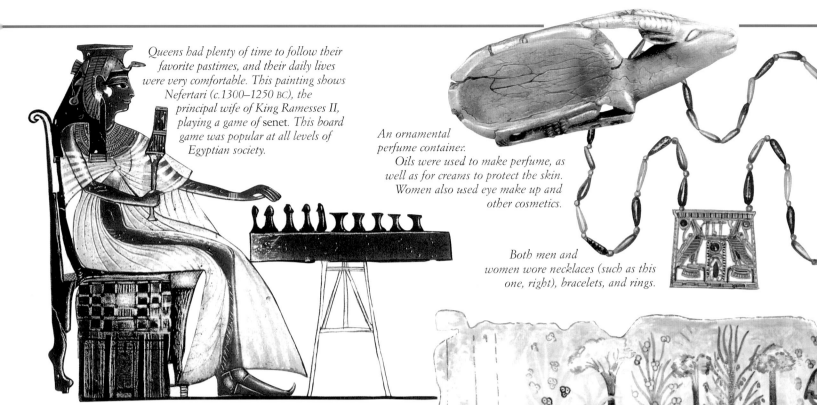

Queens had plenty of time to follow their favorite pastimes, and their daily lives were very comfortable. This painting shows Nefertari (c.1300–1250 BC), the principal wife of King Ramesses II, playing a game of senet. This board game was popular at all levels of Egyptian society.

An ornamental perfume container. Oils were used to make perfume, as well as for creams to protect the skin. Women also used eye make up and other cosmetics.

Both men and women wore necklaces (such as this one, right), bracelets, and rings.

Children's games

Egyptian children had all sorts of toys and games. Babies were given rattles, and older children had spinning tops, and balls made of wood, leather, or reeds. Children of better-off families had wooden toys such as cats or crocodiles with moving jaws, as well as puppets and horses mounted on wheels. Poorer children used mud from the Nile to make their own model animals. Boys played with toy battleaxes, and girls had wooden and rag dolls with their own tiny beds.

Toys were usually buried with children who died young, because the Egyptians believed they could play with them in the next world.

Those who could afford it liked to have a garden beside their house. This was often full of trees, such as sycamore figs and date palms. Some gardens had a pool that was stocked with fish and water lilies.

The Egyptians enjoyed family life, as shown in this wall painting from about 1150 BC. Parents, especially mothers, spent as much time as they could with their children. Egyptian artists always painted children as much smaller than they really were, to show that they were not fully grown.

This statuette of a girl from the early New Kingdom period shows a graceful simplicity.

This small round piece of colored glasswork was used as the whorl on a spindle.

Motherhood

Mothers were honored within the Egyptian family. Their most important task was to bring up their children. Girls stayed at home and helped their mother until they were old enough to get married. They learned many of the things they would need to know when they became mothers. Boys were not with their mothers quite so much: when they were about four years old, their fathers usually started to train them in their own trade.

This woman is being protected and helped in labor by two representatives of the goddess Hathor. Spells and charms were also used to help with safe, easy childbirth.

These guests at a banquet appear in a wall painting from about 1400 BC. They are holding blue lotus flowers. The incense cones that they wore on top of their heavy braided wigs gave off a pleasant fragrance in the warmth of the banqueting room.

Women

Most Egyptian women's lives were spent looking after children and running the family home. Older women helped their daughters and their families. However, Egyptian women did have more freedom and rights than in many later cultures. They could inherit and own property, buy and sell goods, and make their own will. If a man divorced his wife, she kept any valuable possessions that she had brought into the marriage. He also had to give her a share of any property they had bought during their marriage, and then make special payments to her. Women could also divorce men, especially for cruelty. As with men, their daily lives were determined by the class to which they belonged. Royal and high-ranking women had servants – many of whom were female – to look after them. Most ordinary women had a lot of work to do bringing up their family.

Marriage

Girls were often only 12 or 13 when they got married, and their husbands were about 15. Women played a large part in arranging the marriage, and a young man usually asked a female go-between to speak to the girl's mother, rather than to her father. A marriage contract was then drawn up, but there was no wedding ceremony. A newly married couple brought all their possessions to their new home and owned everything jointly. In this statue (left), the husband and wife are shown to be of equal height, suggesting that they had the same status and respect.

Mistress of the house

In large, wealthy households, there were separate living areas for men and women. The mistress of the house might have had her own reception room. She probably had very little housework to do, if any, for a high-ranking woman had plenty of servants for everyday tasks. Servants also helped their mistress with her clothes and make-up, as well as arranging her hair. Less well-off women must have spent much of their time preparing their family's food.

Fertility figurines such as this one were used both at home and in temples. Most homes had a small shrine, where household gods and goddesses were worshiped. In temples, the figurines may have been used by women wishing for a child.

This carving from about 1400 BC shows a mother suckling her baby, who is held tight against her in a wide shawl. Most women breast-fed their children until they were about three, but high-ranking mothers had special nurses to do this for them.

Priestesses

From the Old Kingdom onward, some women from the upper ranks of Egyptian society took part in temple rituals. There were female equivalents to some of the priestly titles held by officials connected with certain temples. Most priestesses were associated with the goddess Hathor, and during worship and ceremonies their main duty was to play a rattle called a *sistrum*. Some women were priestesses of the creator-goddess Neith. It was very rare for a priestess to take part in the cult of a male god.

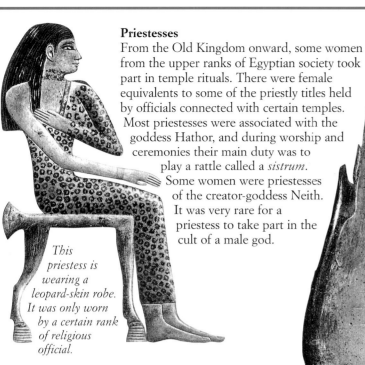

This priestess is wearing a leopard-skin robe. It was only worn by a certain rank of religious official.

Royal women

The most important woman in ancient Egypt was the principal wife of pharaoh (most kings had many wives), who was known as the "great royal wife." Next in importance came the king's mother, and then his other wives. Some queens, such as Hatshepsut, even became "mistress of the two lands" and effectively ruled as pharaoh. They were then looked upon as a king rather than a queen.

Left: Queen Tiye (c.1410–1340 BC), shown left wearing a crown with a raised headdress, was the daughter of a noble military officer. She married King Amenhotep III. When her husband died, Tiye's son Akhenaten became pharaoh and she had great influence as queen mother.

Goddesses

Goddesses were very important to the beliefs and daily lives of the Egyptians, both as wives and mothers of gods and in their own right. Isis (above, left) was the wife of Osiris and the mother of Horus. She was seen as the symbolic mother of the pharaoh himself, and she wore the hieroglyphic sign for throne on her head. Her sister Nephthys (above, right) was called the "lady of the mansion" and wore the hieroglyph sign for this. She was a protector of the dead, and the two goddesses were often portrayed at the head and feet of coffins.

Female dancers were very acrobatic, performing back-bends, handstands, and cartwheels.

Work

Women's work depended on their wealth and social status. In larger, wealthier households there were servants to do everyday jobs, and many of these were women. In smaller houses, the wife and mother had to do these chores herself. Preparing food took up a lot of time, as did spinning, weaving, and the making of clothes. Food was cooked in clay ovens in the courtyard, and some women took a midday meal to their husbands in the fields.

Above: This servant girl is wearing an elaborate collar necklace, a long braided wig, and nothing else. Young women were often shown this way in art, but in real life may have worn clothes.

Clothes

Since the Egyptian climate was hot, most women wore simple, loose-fitting dresses made of linen. During the Old Kingdom, however, many were also shown wearing tighter sheath dresses. By the Middle Kingdom the Egyptians were also dyeing their clothes in colored patterns, as shown by the offering-bearer here.

Women from poorer families also helped with farm work. This woman is sowing seeds in a freshly plowed field.

Below: Women played a wide range of musical instruments, especially during ceremonies and banquets.

Harp   Lute   Flutes   Lyre

The Valley of the Kings

This highly decorated vase topped by a lion was found in the most famous tomb of all, that of Tutankhamun.

Nearly all of the New Kingdom pharaohs starting from Tuthmosis I, who died in 1492 BC, chose to be buried in rock-cut tombs in a valley on the west bank of the Nile, near the ancient city of Thebes. We call this cemetery of 62 tombs the Valley of the Kings. The tombs are made up of corridors and chambers, sloping downward into the cliffs. Their entrances were small in an attempt to conceal them from robbers, but all except one were emptied of their treasures, probably before 1000 BC. The exception was the now famous tomb of Tutankhamun, though that too was robbed in ancient times before being resealed. The last pharaoh buried in the Valley was Ramesses XI, who died in 1070 BC. About 40 mummies of New Kingdom pharaohs, including Seti I and Ramesses II, were moved in about 1000 BC to a site at nearby Deir el-Bahri. Others were discovered in 1898 in the tomb of Amenhotep II in the Valley of the Kings itself.

Amenhotep I, the second pharaoh of the 18th Dynasty, introduced the tradition of having a separate tomb and temple. He founded the tomb-workers' village at Deir el-Medina, but his own original burial place has never been identified. His body was moved about 500 years after burial, and his mummy was discovered in modern times. It is the only royal mummy that has not been unwrapped.

SECOND STAIRCASE

THIRD STAIRCASE

FOURTH STAIRCASE

TOMB OF SETI I

BURIAL CHAMBER

ANTECHAMBER

MUMMY OF SETI I

This diagram of the tomb of Seti I (ruled 1291–78 BC) shows the burial chamber at the end of a long corridor, beyond four sets of stairways. These and the chamber that leads off to the right at the third stairway were an attempt to defeat tomb robbers which failed. Nevertheless, this tomb is the most complete in the entire Valley and has the finest architecture and decoration. It was rediscovered by Giovanni Belzoni in 1817.

The tomb-workers' village

In 1905 the Italian archeologist Ernesto Schiaparelli (1856–1928) began excavating a settlement just to the southeast of the Valley of the Kings. It soon became clear that this was a village that had housed the workmen who cut and decorated the royal tombs, as well as their wives and children. Inscriptions and other evidence showed that a hundred or more people lived in the community, and many of the men and women could clearly read and write. The excavation of their houses has told us a great deal about how ordinary Egyptians lived.

This basket lid, stool, and brush, along with the vase, were found at Deir el-Medina. The vase was made in Mycenae, showing that the tomb-workers were able to afford imported goods.

This senet board-game box was found at Deir el-Medina. It has a drawer for keeping the pieces. The game was for two players, who threw sticks or knucklebones to move their pieces around the board.

The workers' strike

During the reign of Ramesses III massive building works were undertaken on his mortuary temple and tomb. These works put a strain on resources, so administrators decided to cut the grain rations paid to the workers. This resulted in the world's first-known labor dispute, when the workers finally stopped work and marched to one of the royal temples to complain. Priests recorded the complaints and sent them to Thebes, where administrators decided to give out extra rations before the situation got worse.

Reconstruction of a worker's house at Deir el-Medina. The sleeping quarters are on the left, next to a living area with simple furniture. There is also a cellar and, on the far right below ground, a storage room for grain.

Tomb design

No two tombs in the Valley of the Kings are exactly alike. Each one was planned, designed, and decorated in its own unique way, although some features were similar. The basic shape of the tombs changed over time. Early tombs of the 18th Dynasty were curved, so that the corridor turned at right-angles into a pillared hall. Later tombs had just a small kink at this point, and by the 20th Dynasty tombs were quite straight. In all cases the sarcophagus was in a burial chamber, or "house of gold," at the very far end of the tomb.

This painting from the tomb of Ramesses I (ruled 1293–91 BC) shows the 19th-Dynasty king flanked by Horus, the falcon-headed god of the sky, and Anubis, the jackal-headed god of the dead. Ramesses I's tomb is next to that of his son, Seti I, in the middle of the Valley of the Kings.

Decorating the tombs

While a tomb was under construction it must have been very crowded. Excavating, plastering, carving, drawing, and painting all went on at the same time in different parts of the tomb. After wall surfaces had been prepared and plastered, draftsmen sketched vignettes and texts on the walls in red ink. Skilled masons then carved some parts of the drafted designs into raised relief, before painters added bright colors and completed the outlines. Artists worked by the light of linen wicks soaked in fat or oil burning in pottery bowls.

The Valley of the Kings also contains tombs for nobles, courtiers, and the families of pharaohs. This inlaid wooden casket was found in the tomb of Yuya and Tuyu, the parents of Queen Tiye, who was the wife of Amenhotep III.

This wall painting comes from the tomb of Amenherkhepeshef, son of Ramesses III, in the Valley of the Queens. It shows the king in ceremonial dress being led by the goddess Isis.

The Valley of the Queens

Though many rulers' wives were buried in the same tombs as their husbands in the Valley of the Kings, others were buried with their sons in a special nearby cemetery of rock-cut tombs that we call the Valley of the Queens. The earliest tomb is that of Satra, wife of Ramesses I, but the largest and most beautifully decorated is that of Nefertari. In the mid-20th century the tomb's magnificent wall paintings began to suffer serious damage, and they have since been restored.

This scene of the sun-god as a ram-headed falcon comes from the burial chamber of Tawosret, the wife of Seti II. Her tomb was completed by Setnakhte (ruled 1185–82 BC), the first king of the 20th Dynasty. This double tomb in the Valley of the Kings had been robbed and had lain open since ancient times.

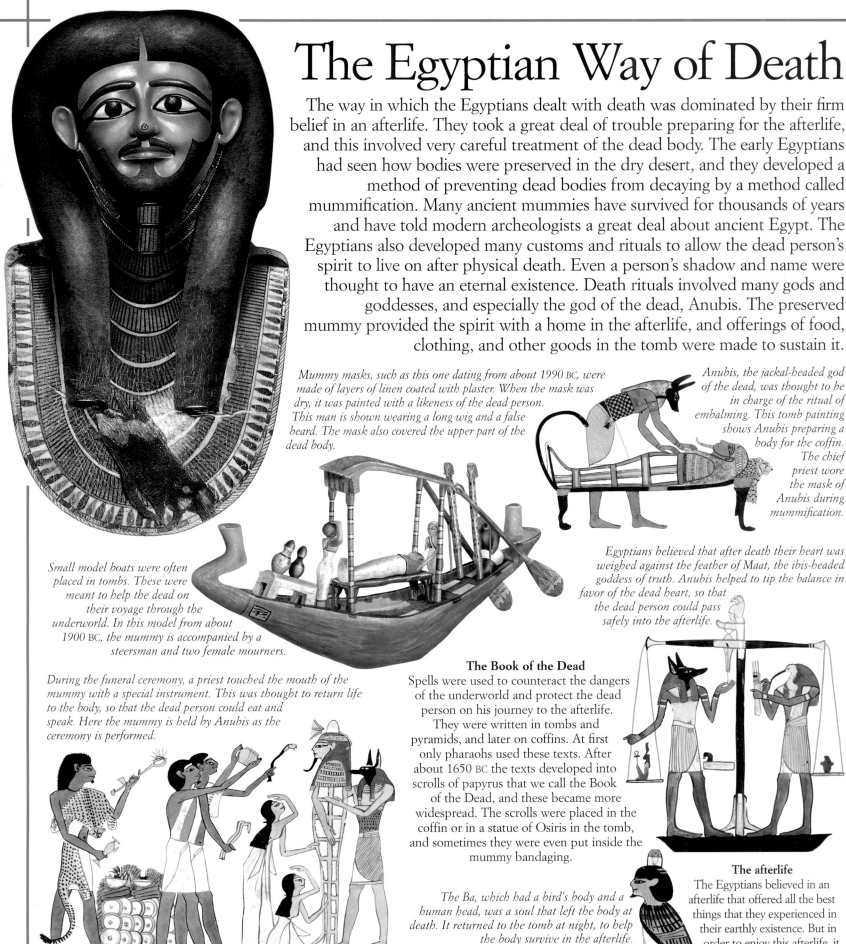

The Egyptian Way of Death

The way in which the Egyptians dealt with death was dominated by their firm belief in an afterlife. They took a great deal of trouble preparing for the afterlife, and this involved very careful treatment of the dead body. The early Egyptians had seen how bodies were preserved in the dry desert, and they developed a method of preventing dead bodies from decaying by a method called mummification. Many ancient mummies have survived for thousands of years and have told modern archeologists a great deal about ancient Egypt. The Egyptians also developed many customs and rituals to allow the dead person's spirit to live on after physical death. Even a person's shadow and name were thought to have an eternal existence. Death rituals involved many gods and goddesses, and especially the god of the dead, Anubis. The preserved mummy provided the spirit with a home in the afterlife, and offerings of food, clothing, and other goods in the tomb were made to sustain it.

Mummy masks, such as this one dating from about 1990 BC, were made of layers of linen coated with plaster. When the mask was dry, it was painted with a likeness of the dead person. This man is shown wearing a long wig and a false beard. The mask also covered the upper part of the dead body.

Anubis, the jackal-headed god of the dead, was thought to be in charge of the ritual of embalming. This tomb painting shows Anubis preparing a body for the coffin. The chief priest wore the mask of Anubis during mummification.

Small model boats were often placed in tombs. These were meant to help the dead on their voyage through the underworld. In this model from about 1900 BC, the mummy is accompanied by a steersman and two female mourners.

Egyptians believed that after death their heart was weighed against the feather of Maat, the ibis-headed goddess of truth. Anubis helped to tip the balance in favor of the dead heart, so that the dead person could pass safely into the afterlife.

During the funeral ceremony, a priest touched the mouth of the mummy with a special instrument. This was thought to return life to the body, so that the dead person could eat and speak. Here the mummy is held by Anubis as the ceremony is performed.

The Book of the Dead
Spells were used to counteract the dangers of the underworld and protect the dead person on his journey to the afterlife. They were written in tombs and pyramids, and later on coffins. At first only pharaohs used these texts. After about 1650 BC the texts developed into scrolls of papyrus that we call the Book of the Dead, and these became more widespread. The scrolls were placed in the coffin or in a statue of Osiris in the tomb, and sometimes they were even put inside the mummy bandaging.

The Ba, which had a bird's body and a human head, was a soul that left the body at death. It returned to the tomb at night, to help the body survive in the afterlife.

The afterlife
The Egyptians believed in an afterlife that offered all the best things that they experienced in their earthly existence. But in order to enjoy this afterlife, it was necessary for all the different parts of a person to continue to exist. The physical body needed to remain intact, the person's name had to continue to exist, and the spirit forms of Ka and Ba had to be supplied with food and drink. Wealthy Egyptians made elaborate preparations for their mummification and tomb, long before they expected to die, to make sure that they could fully enjoy the afterlife.

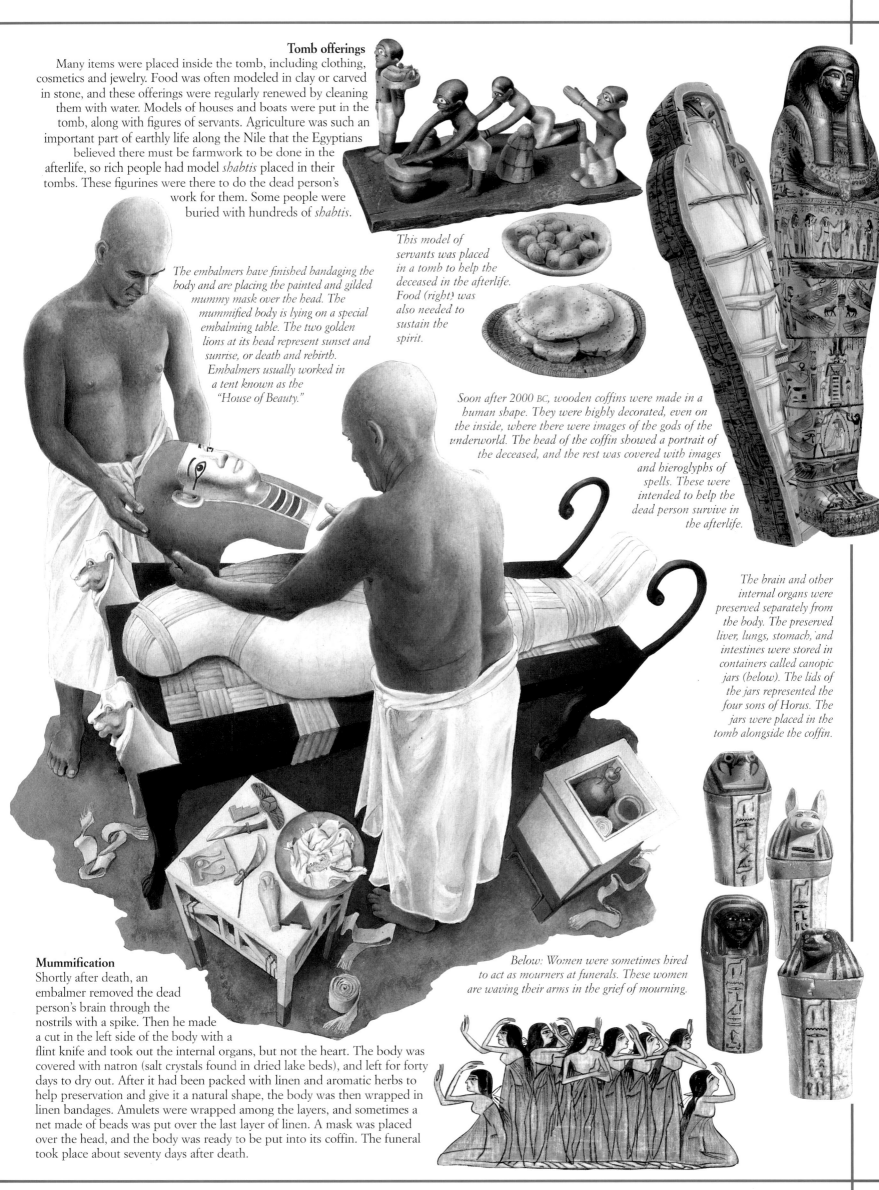

Tomb offerings

Many items were placed inside the tomb, including clothing, cosmetics and jewelry. Food was often modeled in clay or carved in stone, and these offerings were regularly renewed by cleaning them with water. Models of houses and boats were put in the tomb, along with figures of servants. Agriculture was such an important part of earthly life along the Nile that the Egyptians believed there must be farmwork to be done in the afterlife, so rich people had model *shabtis* placed in their tombs. These figurines were there to do the dead person's work for them. Some people were buried with hundreds of *shabtis*.

The embalmers have finished bandaging the body and are placing the painted and gilded mummy mask over the head. The mummified body is lying on a special embalming table. The two golden lions at its head represent sunset and sunrise, or death and rebirth. Embalmers usually worked in a tent known as the "House of Beauty."

This model of servants was placed in a tomb to help the deceased in the afterlife. Food (right) was also needed to sustain the spirit.

Soon after 2000 BC, wooden coffins were made in a human shape. They were highly decorated, even on the inside, where there were images of the gods of the underworld. The head of the coffin showed a portrait of the deceased, and the rest was covered with images and hieroglyphs of spells. These were intended to help the dead person survive in the afterlife.

The brain and other internal organs were preserved separately from the body. The preserved liver, lungs, stomach, and intestines were stored in containers called canopic jars (below). The lids of the jars represented the four sons of Horus. The jars were placed in the tomb alongside the coffin.

Mummification

Shortly after death, an embalmer removed the dead person's brain through the nostrils with a spike. Then he made a cut in the left side of the body with a flint knife and took out the internal organs, but not the heart. The body was covered with natron (salt crystals found in dried lake beds), and left for forty days to dry out. After it had been packed with linen and aromatic herbs to help preservation and give it a natural shape, the body was then wrapped in linen bandages. Amulets were wrapped among the layers, and sometimes a net made of beads was put over the last layer of linen. A mask was placed over the head, and the body was ready to be put into its coffin. The funeral took place about seventy days after death.

Below: Women were sometimes hired to act as mourners at funerals. These women are waving their arms in the grief of mourning.

The Third Intermediate Period

For more than 500 years after the end of the New Kingdom, the balance of power in Egypt was in a constant state of change. We call this time, from 1069 to 525 BC, the Third Intermediate Period. At first the Egyptian kings of the 21st Dynasty, who ruled from the delta town of Tanis, shared power with the High Priests of Amun in Thebes. When a Libyan dynasty took over at Tanis, the Thebans appointed one of their own High Priests as king. They were followed by Kushites, from Nubia, who also worshiped Amun and whose history had been intertwined with that of Egypt for many centuries. The Kushites withdrew when the northern region was attacked by Assyrians, who helped create a new Dynasty of Egyptian kings at Sais, another delta town.

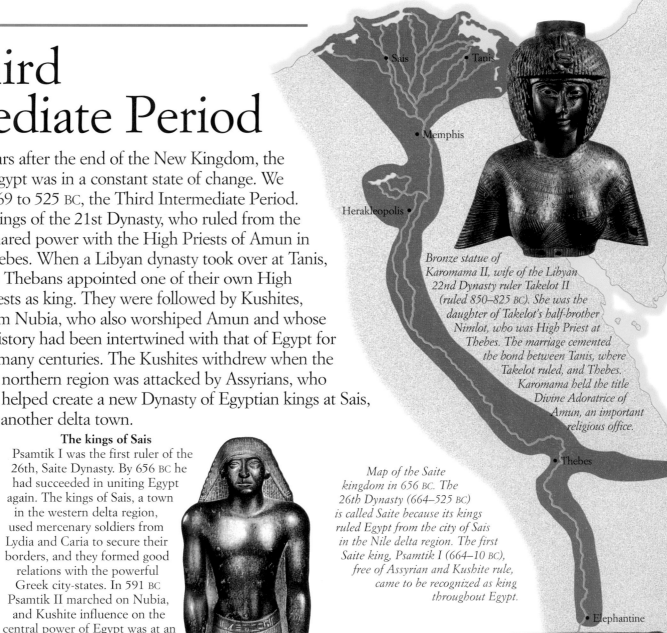

Bronze statue of Karomama II, wife of the Libyan 22nd Dynasty ruler Takelot II (ruled 850–825 BC). She was the daughter of Takelot's half-brother Nimlot, who was High Priest at Thebes. The marriage cemented the bond between Tanis, where Takelot ruled, and Thebes. Karomama held the title Divine Adoratrice of Amun, an important religious office.

The kings of Sais

Psamtik I was the first ruler of the 26th, Saite Dynasty. By 656 BC he had succeeded in uniting Egypt again. The kings of Sais, a town in the western delta region, used mercenary soldiers from Lydia and Caria to secure their borders, and they formed good relations with the powerful Greek city-states. In 591 BC Psamtik II marched on Nubia, and Kushite influence on the central power of Egypt was at an end. The Saites did their best to preserve a delicate balance of power, but were finally conquered by the Persians in 525 BC.

Stone head of Taharqa (690–64 BC), the most important ruler of the 25th, Kushite Dynasty. He defeated the invading Assyrian army in 674 BC, but three years later it returned and drove him out of Memphis.

Map of the Saite kingdom in 656 BC. The 26th Dynasty (664–525 BC) is called Saite because its kings ruled Egypt from the city of Sais in the Nile delta region. The first Saite king, Psamtik I (664–10 BC), free of Assyrian and Kushite rule, came to be recognized as king throughout Egypt.

Granite statue of Mentuemhet (c.700–650 BC), one of the most powerful men in Thebes, who held the offices of "Prince of the City" and "Fourth Prophet of Amun." He saw many changes and maintained his position despite the sacking of Thebes by the Assyrians. His career spanned the 25th and 26th Dynasties.

Left: The Assyrian ruler Ashurbanipal (ruled 668–27 BC), who in 664 BC captured Memphis before sacking Thebes and looting its temples. While Ashurbanipal was active in Egypt, his brother ruled over Babylonia, and finally their rivalry led to war between Assyria and Babylonia.

Detail from the coffin of Nesmut, the musician of Amun, from the early 22nd, Libyan Dynasty. On the left the cobra-goddess Wadjyt wears the red crown of Lower Egypt, balanced on the right by the vulture-goddess Nekhbet and the white crown of Upper Egypt.

Assyrian invasion

In 671 BC the Assyrians, from northeastern Mesopotamia, invaded Egypt. Under their king, Esarhaddon, the Assyrians captured Memphis and most of the royal family except for King Taharqa, who escaped south to Thebes. When the Assyrians withdrew, Taharqa regained power. In 668 BC the Assyrians returned under their new king Ashurbanipal, and this time Taharqa withdrew to the Kushite capital of Napata. Thebes was sacked in 664 BC, and when the new Kushite king Tanutamun withdrew to Nubia once again, the Assyrians made Psamtik governor, and independent ruler of Lower Egypt.

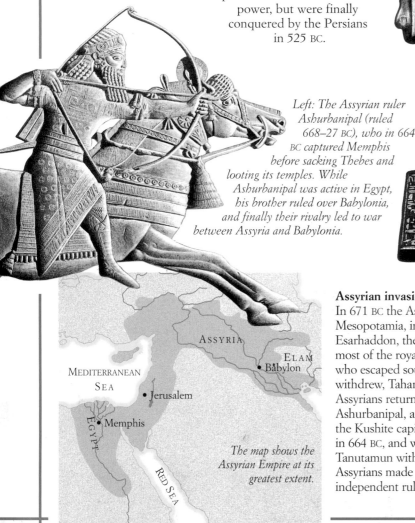

The map shows the Assyrian Empire at its greatest extent.

This painted leather catafalque was used during the 21st Dynasty by the High Priest of Amun, Pinedjem I (1070–32 BC), to hide valuables from tomb robbers.

The rule of the Kushites

The Egyptians had had dealings with the southern region of Nubia, including what the Egyptians called the Kingdom of Kush, for centuries. Since the 18th Dynasty the pharaoh had been represented there by his own Viceroy of Kush. The local Kushite rulers at Napata used the divisions within Egypt during the 24th Dynasty to gain control of Lower Nubia and then gain acceptance by the ruling families of Thebes. However, the 25th, Kushite Dynasty lasted for less than a hundred years.

Alabaster statue of Amenirdis I, sister of 25th-Dynasty King Shabaka (ruled 716–702 BC) and daughter of the Kushite ruler Kashta. Amenirdis was officially adopted by the holder of the office of "God's Wife of Amun," which helped give the Kushites control in Thebes.

Statue of the last Saite Dynasty ruler, Psamtik III (ruled 526–525 BC). He is shown with the goddess Hathor, who was regarded as the divine mother of the reigning king. Psamtik was executed by the Persian ruler Cambyses, who invaded Egypt in 525 BC.

The Libyan princes

During the 21st Dynasty the royalty at Tanis married more and more members of the Libyan nobility, who had been living for a long time in Egypt. In 945 BC Sheshonq I founded the 22nd Dynasty, and Libyan chiefs ruled Egypt for the next 200 years. Sheshonq ruled from Tanis, but he made one of his sons High Priest at Thebes, where the earlier priests were losing their power, and another Libyan relative became prince of Herakleopolis. In this way a certain unity returned to Egypt during this so-called Libyan Dynasty.

High Priests at Thebes

At Thebes there was a ruling class of High Priests who were extremely powerful. They owned most of the temple land in Egypt, as well as almost all the ships. The Theban High Priests of Amun were military leaders who defended their interests by building a chain of fortresses to the north of Thebes. They acquired supposedly divine decisions through oracles and used these to make their actions official. Together with their great power in the Theban region, the priests had contact with the delta pharaohs at Tanis, and the office of "god's wife of Amun" was often held by northern princesses.

This gold and silver bowl with a glass rosette in the center was part of the funerary treasure of Wendjebauendjed, a general and high priest of the 21st Dynasty. The general was held in such high regard by King Psusennes I that he was buried in the royal tomb at Tanis.

Gold funeral mask (left) of Sheshonq II. He ruled as co-regent with his father, the 22nd-Dynasty ruler Osorkon I (ruled 924–889 BC), but died before he could become king himself.

Tanis

At the start of the Third Intermediate Period there were two distinct centers of power in Egypt – Thebes and Tanis. The first king of the 21st Dynasty, Smendes I (ruled 1069–1043 BC), made his capital at Tanis, in the delta region. Many monuments from Middle and New Kingdom times were moved from other sites, and Tanis became a great city of obelisks. There were still strong links with Thebes, and a temple was dedicated at Tanis to the Theban trio of deities – Amun, Mut, and Khons.

The royal tombs of Tanis were rediscovered in 1939 and included the tomb of Psusennes I (ruled 1039–991 BC), which was found totally intact.

Silver coffin of Psusennes I, overlaid with gold, which was found in one of six tombs at Tanis discovered by Pierre Montet in 1939. Silver was rarer than gold in Egypt, and this coffin was therefore extremely valuable.

Darius I (ruled 521–486 BC) succeeded Cambyses II as king of Persia in 522 BC and was forced to deal with revolts throughout the Persian empire. He undertook a great deal of building work in Egypt, finishing some projects that had been started by the kings of Sais. He also completed a canal from the eastern delta of the Nile to the Red Sea.

The temple of Isis and other smaller buildings on Agilkia Island in the Nile River, just south of Aswan. The temple was first built around 380 BC, and the remains were moved from the nearby island of Philae before it was submerged after construction of the Aswan High Dam in the 1960s.

The Late Period

In 539 BC the Persian king Cyrus the Great conquered Babylonia and created a larger empire than the world had ever known. Just 14 years later, Cyrus's son Cambyses II expanded the empire even farther by conquering Egypt. This was the start of the so-called Late Period. From 525 BC until 332 BC, when the Persians were finally driven out, the Egyptians were forced to endure two dynasties of Persian rulers. The invaders even introduced a new language and script, Aramaic. When they were not under direct rule, three short dynasties of Egyptian kings in the Nile delta region had to be constantly on the lookout for another Persian invasion. Nevertheless, a considerable amount of building work was undertaken during these troubled times. The Late Period came to an end when the Macedonians drove out and replaced the Persians.

The cult of the Apis bull, the god Ptah in animal form, was still popular in the Late Period. The Greek writer Herodotus wrote that the first Persian ruler killed the Apis bull; perhaps this was an attempt to discredit the Persians.

This stone statue shows the falcon-god Horus towering over and protecting the small figure of Nakhtnebef (ruled 380–362 BC), the first king of the 30th Dynasty. In earlier times statues showed the proportions between god and king the other way round.

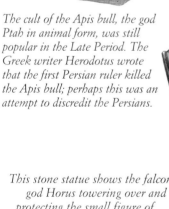

Statue of the creator-god Ptah, who wears a skull-cap on his shaved head. Ptah was associated with craftsmen, and the High Priest of Ptah also held the title "supreme leader of craftsmen." Ptah was believed to have created the world with thoughts from his heart and words from his tongue. He was widely worshiped during the Late Period.

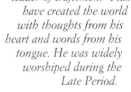

Stone head of Nakhtnebef from around 370 BC, showing the typical features of statues at that time. Nakhtnebef came from a military family and succeeded in driving out invading Persians from the delta region in 373 BC.

The First Persian Period

The 27th Dynasty of rulers of Egypt was made up of six Persian kings. This period, which lasted for more than 100 years after the Persian invasion of Egypt in 525 BC, is known as the First Persian Period. Some of the Persian rulers furthered Egyptian traditions in both religion and art. The most famous of them, Darius I, built a temple to Amun in the Kharga oasis and helped Egypt remain stable and prosperous. After his death there were several uprisings, and in 404 BC Amyrtaeus, Prince of Sais, declared himself king and succeeded in extending his rule as far south as Aswan.

The dwarf-god Bes was associated with feasting, children, and childbirth, and was seen as a protector of the family. His strange, ugly appearance was perhaps helpful in scaring off evil spirits, and he was thought to keep snakes away from the house.

This dish is covered in Aramaic script. Under Darius I Aramaic became the official language throughout the whole of the Persian Empire. Its 22-character alphabet is the forerunner of both the Hebrew and Arabic alphabets.

This bronze statuette of the cat-goddess Bastet shows her with the body of a woman carrying a basket and looking quite domestic. The goddess's name means "she of the bast (ointment jar)."

Late gods and goddesses

However they felt about it, the Persian invaders were largely powerless to stop the Egyptians upholding many of their traditions. They certainly carried on worshiping their ancient gods and goddesses. The dwarf-god Bes had been important since at least the Middle Kingdom period, and he was still being worshiped after the Persians had been ousted. The cat-goddess Bastet had already been known for over 2,000 years, and during the Late Period she was often portrayed as a family goddess with kittens at her feet. Sacred animals such as the Apis and Buchis bulls were also important cults at this time.

Delta dynasties

After the brief reign of Amyrtaeus (ruled 404–399 BC), the capital moved within the delta region from Sais to Mendes. The first king of the 29th Dynasty to rule there was Nefaarud I (ruled 399–93), who maintained the cult of the sacred Apis bull at Memphis. His successor, Hakor (ruled 393–80 BC), had to fight off several Persian attacks with the help of Greek mercenaries in the Egyptian navy. In 380 BC the next king, Nakhtnebef, moved the capital to another delta city, Sebennytos. His new dynasty lasted just 37 years, however, before the Persians reconquered Egypt.

Greek travelers arrived in Egypt during the second half of the 5th century BC. They included the great historian Herodotus (see page 58), whose writings have been an important source of information about Egyptian life at that time.

During the reign of Djedhor (ruled 362–60 BC), special gold coins were minted at Memphis to pay the Greek mercenaries from Athens and Sparta who helped the Egyptian army against the Persians. The coins were based on the Greek stater, since Egyptian coins were only introduced later.

Coin showing Darius I going into battle.

The Second Persian Period

After the reconquest in 343 BC, three Persians ruled Egypt for just a decade. From later Greek accounts it appears that this Second Persian Period was a harsh one for the Egyptians. Cities were neglected, temples were robbed of their treasures, sacred animals such as the Apis bull were slaughtered, and the people were heavily taxed. This was an unhappy period for Egypt and perhaps explains why Alexander the Great found it so easy to march in and put an end to it in 332 BC.

This detail from a frieze shows one of the highly trained Persian soldiers who were known as the "immortals." There were 10,000 of these elite troops, and as soon as one man died he was replaced.

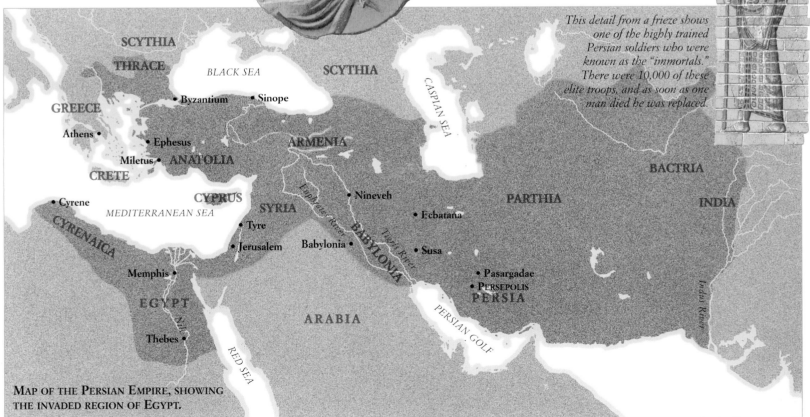

MAP OF THE PERSIAN EMPIRE, SHOWING THE INVADED REGION OF EGYPT.

Greek and Roman Egypt

Alexander the Great added Egypt to his empire in 332 BC and declared himself the son of Amun-Ra and pharaoh. After Alexander's death, his Macedonian dynasty was succeeded by the first Ptolemy. Fourteen further Ptolemies later spread Greek culture throughout Egypt, where the official languages became Greek and, for ordinary people, Demotic. The country now had a money-based economy, new reservoirs meant that more than one harvest a year could be gathered, and Egypt's population grew to a total of more than five million. During the 2nd and 1st centuries BC, however, Egypt fell under the influence of Rome, and it became part of the Roman Empire in 30 BC. During the Roman period Christianity began to rival the cults of Egyptian gods, and when Roman rule ended, large parts of Egypt converted to Christianity. This so-called Coptic period lasted until the Islamic invasion of AD 642.

The Pharos of Alexandria, the world's first lighthouse and one of the Seven Wonders of the Ancient World. It took about 15 years to build and was completed around 283 BC under Ptolemy II (ruled 285–46 BC). About 440 feet tall, the lighthouse had a fire at the top that was reflected by polished bronze mirrors, and it was used to guide ships safely into the harbor of Alexandria.

Marble bust of Cleopatra VII (69–30 BC), who was the last and most famous of seven Ptolemaic queens of Egypt given the name Cleopatra. She first shared the co-regency of Egypt with her father, Ptolemy XII, and then with her brother, Ptolemy XIII. She was supported by the Roman general, Julius Caesar, who she claimed was the father of her son, Ptolemy Caesarion.

The Ptolemaic period

This period began when the Macedonian troops of Alexander the Great marched into Memphis in 332 BC, and it lasted for just over 300 years. Alexander had himself confirmed King of Egypt by the oracle of Amun at Siwa oasis. When Alexander died in 323 BC, his generals divided his huge empire and Ptolemy gained control of Egypt. Eighteen years later Ptolemy took the title of king and founded the dynasty known as the Ptolemies. The city of Alexandria became Egypt's capital, and its magnificent library and museum made the city a great cultural center. The Ptolemies spread Greek culture, but they also rebuilt temples to Egyptian gods and increased foreign trade. Their rule lasted until 30 BC.

Coin showing the head of Ptolemy I (ruled 305–285 BC), the founder of the Ptolemaic line who came to the throne of Egypt 18 years after the death of Alexander the Great. He introduced the cult of the god Serapis, combining Osiris-Apis with Greek gods such as Zeus.

This bust of an early Ptolemaic ruler shows the typical qualities of Egyptian sculpture. The Ptolemies had their wives declared queens and insisted that they and all previous kings and queens of their dynasty be worshiped by the people.

Green schist head from Alexandria, dating from the rule of Ptolemy XII (ruled 80–51 BC).

Ptolemaic rulers adopted many Egyptian ceremonies. This stela of Ptolemy V (ruled 205–180 BC) shows the king making an offering to the sacred bull Buchis. The bull's body is covered in gold leaf, and on its head it wears the emblem of Montu, the god of war. Montu was worshiped from the Middle Kingdom right through to the Roman period, being combined with the sun-god as Montu-Ra.

This glass goblet dating from the 3rd century AD was among many objects found at the religious site of Sedeinga in Upper Nubia. A Greek inscription runs round the top of the glass.

During the Roman period Egyptian mummies reflected Roman art and fashion. This mummy mask, dating from the early 1st century AD, has imitation hair made of dyed cotton. The woman wears earrings, bracelets and a glass necklace, as well as a wreath of blossoms made of fine plaster leaves. The pictorial frieze behind her head is in a traditional Egyptian style.

The style of this decoration from a linen shroud from the 3rd century AD shows a Roman influence. The shroud was used to wrap a mummy. It shows Anubis, the god of the dead, attending to the deceased, who is standing next to his own mummy.

The Roman period

In 31 BC the navy of Mark Antony, a co-ruler of Rome and supporter of the Ptolemaic queen Cleopatra VII, lost the Battle of Actium to Octavian's fleet. The following year Octavian (later known as Augustus) appointed himself pharaoh and made Egypt his imperial estate, effectively a province of Rome. Over the next 425 years, Egypt was ruled by more than 50 successive Roman emperors. There was no ruling family in Egypt, however, and the Romans saw the country principally as a rich source of grain and gold Few emperors took an interest in Egypt or visited the province, and this period ended in 395 AD when the Roman Empire was split into East and West.

This cult statuette of Aphrodite, the Greek goddess of love who was worshiped as the "queen of heaven," was found in an Egyptian tomb. The statuette was probably used for worship at home and dates from the Roman period. The Roman goddess Venus was associated with Aphrodite.

This marble foot from Alexandria dates from the Roman period. As a votive object it was associated with leaving footprints at temples to record visits or pilgrimages. The foot shows the figures of the deities Serapis and Isis, who represented the natural forces of male and female fertility, as human-headed serpents. On the heel is Harpocrates, a later form of the god Horus.

Coptic tapestry roundel made of linen and wool. Many such fabrics, as well as silk items, were found in cemeteries of the Christian period at Akhmim, a town on the east bank of the Nile that was the capital of the 9th nome of Upper Egypt.

Bronze statuette of a horseman carrying a cross, dating from around the 7th century AD, the end of the Coptic period. The Egyptian Copts made their greatest contribution to Christianity when Anthony of Thebes (AD 251–356), who spent 20 years alone in the wilderness, founded the Christian monastic movement.

The Coptic period

From the split of the Roman Empire in AD 395 to the Islamic conquest of 642, Egypt was controlled from Byzantium. This period in Egyptian history is known as the Coptic or Christian period. The Christian church had been founded in Egypt by the apostle Mark in AD 70, but few Egyptians converted to Christianity before the 3rd century AD. Then the ideal of the monastic way of life was founded in Egypt by Anthony of Thebes. The new Coptic Church added some demotic signs to the Greek alphabet to cover Egyptian sounds and create a new script. By the 6th century paganism was formally ended, and the temple of Isis at Philae was closed in 536. During the following century Arab armies invaded Egypt and drove out the Byzantine troops. Islamic rule was established in 642.

Panel from a 4th century AD wooden chest inlaid with ivory. This and similar objects were found at Qustul, a funeral site on the upper Nile near the temple of Abu Simbel.

This beautiful lioness's head is made of gilded wood, inlaid with blue and black glass. It was part of a couch found in the tomb of Tutankhamun.

Medium-sized wild cats are shown on some ancient reliefs. One was the caracal, or desert lynx, with its distinctive black ear tufts. This animal is now rare in the region.

Animals

Animals formed an important part of the ancient Egyptian world. There were many wild animals on the edge of the desert, in the marshlands near the banks of the Nile, and in the river itself. Some, such as lions and crocodiles, were feared, while large beasts such as the hippopotamus caused great damage to crops. Hunting was important, in early times as a source of food and later as sport. Cattle, sheep, goats, and other animals were domesticated and farmed for their meat, milk, hide, and wool. Smaller animals such as dogs, cats and monkeys were kept as pets, and were very popular with children. Most importantly, Egyptian animals were associated with gods and goddesses, as well as ancient beliefs and myths, and this lent them an added significance.

Lions and kings
The connection between Egyptian kings and lions may have come about when predynastic tribal chiefs started hunting the big cats and admired their aggression. In ancient times lions lived near the edge of the deserts near the Nile. They were seen as guardians of the eastern and western horizons and therefore of sunrise and sunset.

Changing times
Many of the region's wild animals, such as the desert lynx, were more common in ancient times than they are today. The Barbary sheep, which ranged throughout the dry, rocky regions in ancient times, is also rare in modern Egypt. Rams with corkscrew horns (right) had little fleece, and by the Middle Kingdom had been replaced with a more wooly variety of sheep. Nevertheless, the earlier rams – and especially their horns – were still used as symbols of gods and kings.

The world's smallest fox, the fennec, lives in the deserts of north Africa. Its distinctive large ears allow it to lose heat quickly. It shelters in a burrow during the day and comes out to feed at night.

A mummy with a ram's head, supporting the sun on its horns. This represents the union of the gods Ra and Osiris.

This bronze cat represents the living form of the goddess Bastet. She wears the sacred eye of Horus on her chest, a gold nose-ring and gold earrings. The eyes were originally inlaid.

A gilded wooden and bronze statue of a sacred Ibis representing Thoth, the god of writing and knowledge. Maat, the goddess of truth and order, is squatting before the bird.

The owl stood for the letter "m" in the Egyptians' hieroglyphic script. This sign is unusual, because few Egyptian drawings showed an animal looking straight at the observer.

Sacred animals
The Egyptians regarded many animals as sacred. The falcon was sacred to the gods Horus and Osiris, the ibis to Thoth, the cat to the goddess Bastet, the cow to Hathor, and the crocodile to Sobek. Some gods were linked to more than one animal. The goddess Serket, for example, often featured in spells to cure poisonous bites and was associated with scorpions and snakes, as well as lionesses. The sacred Apis bull (see opposite page) was an individual animal rather than a group or species of animals.

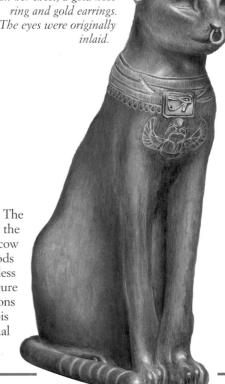

This statuette of a hippopotamus is decorated with some of the plants that grew around the Nile marshes. Hippos caused damage and were feared by the Egyptians, but they have since died out in the region.

Egyptian scribes used animals as characters to illustrate a moral. This papyrus painting shows a lion sitting down with an antelope to play the board game called senet. The two animals were natural enemies, and it looks as if the predator is about to triumph over its prey.

Art and sculpture

In Egyptian art, animals usually represented gods or people. Falcons and lions represented the pharaoh and showed his connection to important gods such as Horus and Sekhmet. The cobra was a sacred image of Wadjyt, a goddess of Lower Egypt, while Upper Egypt was represented by Nekhbet and her vulture. As ruler of both kingdoms, the pharaoh had both animals on his headdress. Animal figurines (such as the hippopotamus above) were often included in human burials, to help protect the dead.

Sacred cats were mummified and put in plaster, wooden, or stone coffins. The Egyptians believed that the cats would live again and serve as agents between their gods and humans.

Burial and offerings

All sorts of animals were embalmed and buried as mummies. Remains have been found of falcons, cats, dogs, crocodiles, rams, baboons, snakes, mongooses, fishes, and even beetles. At Saqqara up to four million mummified sacred ibises were placed in pottery jars and lined up in neat rows. Some of these animals may have had a natural death, but many were specially raised and then killed so that their mummies could be offered by temple devotees to the gods to which the animals were sacred. When a temple was overflowing with animal mummies, they were taken away and buried in a nearby cemetery.

The sacred Apis bull was an individual living animal, specially selected to be the earthly form of the god Ptah. When the bull died, it was embalmed and its mummy was taken from Memphis to Saqqara for burial in a granite sarcophagus. A new bull with the right markings was then chosen.

This painting from around 1400 BC shows the scribe Nebamun hunting birds from a reed boat in the Nile marshes. He holds a throwing stick in one hand, and decoy herons in the other. He is accompanied by his wife, daughter, pet cat, and goose.

Hunting

The earliest Egyptians lived by hunting and gathering along the banks of the River Nile. When their ancestors settled in farming villages, the hunting traditions continued and formed a welcome extra source of food. For the richer members of Egyptian society, hunting became a favorite pastime. Lions and wild deer were hunted in the desert, and hippopotamuses and crocodiles in the marshes. Hunting parties for hippos were made up of many boats, and the animals were killed with spears. Birds were knocked down with throwing sticks and caught in nets. By the time of the New Kingdom, the pharaoh himself took part in hunting big game such as lions, elephants, and rhinoceroses, and the royal hunt became a symbol of kingship to the people of Egypt.

Rediscovering Egypt

During the Roman, Coptic, and Islamic periods of Egyptian history, European scholars began to take an interest in the ancient history of the region. At the same time, however, the sort of first-hand knowledge that is handed down from generation to generation was being lost by Egyptians themselves. The last known hieroglyphic inscription was written in AD 394, and it was almost another 1,500 years before this ancient Egyptian form of writing was deciphered, by Frenchman Jean-François Champollion in 1822. By that time many ancient sites had been rediscovered, and a few decades later an organization was set up to look after Egyptian antiquities. The study of Egyptology grew quickly, and the general public's interest was awakened by the amazing finds at Tutankhamun's tomb in 1922. Today, discoveries are still being made as we learn even more about the ancient Egyptians and their remarkable civilization.

Herodotus (c. 484–20 BC), the first Greek historian, wrote in a lively style about his travels in Egypt during the 27th Dynasty of the Late Period. His work inspired many later historians and geographers.

The Classical world

When Greek and Roman writers traveled to Egypt, they naturally took a great interest in the monuments of the ancient civilization that had developed there. Following in the footsteps of Herodotus (see above), these writers included Diodorus (1st century BC) and the historian and geographer Strabo (c.63 BC–AD 21), who first recorded the use of the Nilometer at Elephantine. The famous Greek biographer and essayist Plutarch (c.AD 46–126) also visited Egypt and wrote a famous account of the myth of Horus and Seth. Throughout the Roman Empire, the spreading cult of the goddess Isis increased interest in other aspects of ancient Egypt, and some antiquities were transported to Rome.

Giovanni Belzoni (1778–1823) was an Italian explorer who found and transported large numbers of Egyptian antiquities for European collectors and museums. He discovered the tomb of King Seti I at western Thebes and the Greco-Roman city of Berenice. By modern standards his methods were unusual, but he noted details of the origin of all the objects he moved and kept good records.

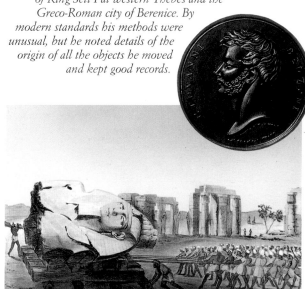

In 1816 Belzoni's workers removed the "young Memnon," part of a colossal statue of Ramesses II, from Luxor on behalf of the British Consul-General in Egypt. The statue became one of the first major Egyptian antiquities in the collection of the British Museum in London.

Englishman Howard Carter (1874–1939) was only 17 years old when he went on an archeological survey of Egypt with the famous Egyptologist Flinders Petrie. In 1922 he made his most famous find – the tomb of Tutankhamun.

Tomb robbery

Tomb robbers have always presented a great problem to archeologists. Some Egyptian tombs were robbed in ancient times or many centuries ago, and modern archeologists have frequently been disappointed when entering a rediscovered tomb or temple to find that it was cleared many years ago of its treasures. Egyptologists such as Howard Carter had to take great care to guard their work-sites during excavation, and it was often difficult to find secure storage for found objects before they were transferred to a museum. Today the trade in antiquities is better controlled, though archeologists must still take great care when they begin work at a new site.

Huge crowds gathered to watch the wonderful objects from Tutankhamun's tomb being removed from the Valley of the Kings. They were taken to Cairo Museum, where they are still on display today.

Mehemet Ali (1769–1849) was viceroy of Egypt for the Ottoman Empire from 1805 to 1848 and is considered to be the founder of modern Egypt. He used European advisers to help modernize the country, increasing its wealth and power. He was open toward the West and allowed European archeologists access to Egyptian antiquities.

Tourism

In the 19th and early 20th centuries, when tourists started visiting ancient sites in Egypt, there were few controls. Sites were damaged by people walking over monuments, touching and moving objects. Many artifacts were then removed to museums, where they were more secure but could still be seen by millions. Today, an entire sector of the tourist industry is devoted to visiting ancient wonders, combined with a boat trip up the Nile. This puts great strain on sites such as Giza, but it is important that people are allowed to enjoy their heritage from the ancient world.

This 1920s' poster advertizes the wonders of a trip down the Nile and a visit to the pyramids. In those days such exotic tourist trips were mainly for the wealthy few.

British Egyptologist Sir John Gardner Wilkinson (1797–1875) first traveled to Egypt in 1821. He spent the next 12 years discovering and studying ancient sites. He made copious notes and drawings at Karnak and the Valley of the Kings, and kept excellent records of his excavations at Thebes. In 1841 he completed his famous three-volume work Manners and Customs of the Ancient Egyptians.

Archeology in the 21st century

We have rediscovered a great deal about Ancient Egypt in the past few centuries, and the work continues. Modern Egyptologists have many aids that their predecessors did not: they can study detailed aerial and satellite photographs of sites and regions; they have sophisticated scanners to investigate mummies; and they can use computers to generate reconstructions of buildings and monuments and see what they actually looked like thousands of years ago. Modern archeologists use nondestructive techniques and whenever possible leave antiquities as they were when they were discovered.

This 1st-century zodiac of the heavens, from the ceiling of the chapel of Osiris in the temple of Hathor at Dendera, was removed during Napoleon's Nile campaign and can be seen in the Louvre museum in Paris. It has been replaced by a copy at Dendera.

The mummy of a young girl found in the late 1990s at Kharga oasis, in the Libyan Desert about 110 miles west of the River Nile. Many mummies have been found in the remains of a peasant village there, dating from the 1st to 3rd century AD. The villagers were poor, but their belief in life after death was strong enough to make them mummify their dead.

Modern archeologists study the temple of Amun at Karnak. Epigraphers make accurate copies of inscriptions, paintings, and reliefs at their original location. Along with photographs, these copies make up an accurate record for others to study.

The growth of Egyptology

In 1858 the governor of Egypt appointed a French Egyptologist, Auguste Mariette (1821–81), to oversee all archeological excavation. Mariette became the first director of the Egyptian Antiquities Service and established a national museum. Excavations became more orderly and were better recorded, and academic posts in Egyptology were created around the world. This paved the way for scholars such as the British archeologist Flinders Petrie (1853–1942) and American George Reisner (1867–1942), who was Professor of Egyptology at Harvard University for 28 years. By the beginning of the 20th century, Egyptology was recognized as an important academic subject.

Scottish painter David Roberts (1796–1864) made detailed sketches of ancient monuments and sites in Egypt in 1838. His beautiful pictures have been useful to later scientists as an accurate record of the sites at that time, before they were further disturbed and uncovered by archeologists.

Napoleon's Nile campaign

In 1798 the great French commander Napoleon Bonaparte sailed for Egypt with about 38,000 troops. His aim was to destroy British trade with the Middle East and block the trade route to India. With his army Napoleon took a group of 167 scholars – botanists, architects, geologists, chemists, and artists – whose task was to collect and record information on all aspects of Egypt, including its ancient history. This they achieved. After success at the Battle of the Pyramids, Napoleon's fleet was defeated just 11 days later at the Battle of the Nile by the British under Admiral Nelson. The scholars, however, were allowed to continue their work until 1802.

Painting by Jean-Antoine Gros of Napoleon at the Battle of the Pyramids in 1798. Napoleon defeated the Mameluke rulers of Egypt to take Cairo and gain control of the country.

Some of the scholars who went on Napoleon's expedition examine ancient monuments and buildings. French artists made superb sketches and paintings of the discoveries, which were published in Paris as a 24-volume series between 1809 and 1822.

Index